Critical Acclaim for Books by Gen and Kelly Tanabe
Authors of *Get into Any College, Get Free Cash for College*
and *1001 Ways to Pay for College*

"Upbeat, well-organized and engaging, this comprehensive tool is an exceptional investment for the college-bound."
—PUBLISHERS WEEKLY

"Helps college applicants write better essays."
—THE DAILY NEWS

"Invaluable information."
—LEONARD BANKS, THE JOURNAL PRESS

"A present for anxious parents."
—MARY KAYE RITZ, THE HONOLULU ADVERTISER

"Helpful, well-organized guide, with copies of actual letters and essays and practical tips. A good resource for all students."
—KLIATT

"When you consider the costs of a four-year college or university education nowadays, think about forking out (the price) for this little gem written and produced by two who know."
—DON DENEVI, PALO ALTO DAILY NEWS

"What's even better than all the top-notch tips is that the book is written in a cool, conversational way."
—COLLEGE BOUND MAGAZINE

"Offers advice on writing a good entrance essay, taking exams and applying for scholarships, and other information on the college experience—start to finish."
—TOWN & COUNTRY MAGAZINE

"I recently applied to Cornell University. I read your book from cover to back, wrote an essay about 'Snorkeling in Okinawa' (which most people criticized), and got ACCEPTED to Cornell. Thank you very much for your help, and I'll be sure to refer this book to anyone applying to college."
—JASON CLEMMEY

"If you're struggling with your essays, the Tanabes offer some encouragement."

—College Bound Magazine

"A 'must' for any prospective college student."

—Midwest Book Review

"The Tanabes literally wrote the book on the topic."

—Bull & Bear Financial Report

"Filled with student-tested strategies."

—Pam Costa, Santa Clara Vision

"Actually shows you how to get into college."

—New Jersey Spectator Leader

"Upbeat tone and clear, practical advice."

—Book News

50 Successful
STANFORD
Application
Essays

SECOND EDITION

Includes advice from Stanford admissions
officers and the 25 essay mistakes that
guarantee failure

GEN and KELLY TANABE

HARVARD GRADUATES AND AUTHORS OF
50 Successful Ivy League Application Essays,
Accepted! 50 Successful College Admission Essays and
The Ultimate Scholarship Book

50 Successful Stanford Application Essays Second Edition
By Gen and Kelly Tanabe

Published by SuperCollege, LLC
2713 Newlands Avenue | Belmont, CA 94002 | www.supercollege.com

Credits: Cover: TLC Graphics, www.TLCGraphics.com. Design: Monica Thomas. Cover photo: © Cupertino10 | Dreamstime.com
Layout: The Roberts Group, www.editorialservice.com

ISBN13: 978-1-61760-094-4
Manufactured in the United States of America
10 9 8 7 6 5 4 3 2 1

Library of Congress Cataloging-in-Publication Data
Names: Tanabe, Gen S. | Tanabe, Kelly Y.
Title: 50 successful Stanford application essays : get into Stanford and
  other top colleges / Gen Tanabe, Kelly Tanabe.
Other titles: Fifty successful Stanford application essays
Description: Second edition. | Belmont, CA : SuperCollege, 2016.
Identifiers: LCCN 2015044678 (print) | LCCN 2015045257 (ebook) | ISBN
  9781617600944 (paperback) | ISBN 9781617601040 (Epub) | ISBN 9781617601057
  (Mobi)
Subjects: LCSH: College applications--California--Palo Alto. | College
  applications--United States. | Stanford University--Admission. |
  Universities and colleges--United States--Admission. | Exposition
  (Rhetoric) | BISAC: STUDY AIDS / College Entrance.
Classification: LCC LB2351.52.U6 T366 2016 (print) | LCC LB2351.52.U6 (ebook)
  | DDC 378.1/616--dc23
LC record available at http://lccn.loc.gov/2015044678

TABLE OF CONTENTS

DEDICATION

To our readers—
WE HOPE YOU ACHIEVE YOUR DREAM!

ACKNOWLEDGMENTS

THIS BOOK WOULD NOT HAVE BEEN possible without the generous contributions of the Stanford students who agreed to share their admissions essays and advice in order to help others who hope to follow in their footsteps.

We would also like to thank the former Stanford admissions officers for spending the time to impart some of their knowledge to our readers: Jon Reider and Irena Smith.

We would like to express our deepest appreciation to contributing writer Elizabeth Soltan.

Special thanks to Chanda Feldman, Alice Hu, Mark Fujiwara, Feyi Lawoyin, Laura Malkiewich and Gregory Yee.

1

25 ESSAY MISTAKES THAT GUARANTEE FAILURE

FOR EVERY OPEN SLOT AT STANFORD, there are about 15 eager applicants vying for it–and you're one of them. On paper, most applicants appear very similar. All are well qualified academically with high grades and test scores and solid involvement in extracurricular activities.

Imagine the admissions officer who must choose which of these well-deserving applications to accept. How will he or she make the decision? Very often, the essay makes a difference. The essay is the one chance for you to share a piece of yourself that is not encapsulated in the dry numbers and scores of the application. It is your opportunity to demonstrate why you'd be a perfect fit at the college, how you'd contribute to the student body and why the college should accept you over those other 14 applicants.

The essay is also the one part of your application that you have complete control over. You can write it the night before it's due and turn in a piece that is half-baked, or you can spend a little time on the essay and turn in one that can set you apart from the competition.

The truth is that you don't have to be a good writer to create a successful admissions essay. Nor do you need to have survived a life changing event or won a Nobel Prize. Writing a successful admissions essay for Stanford is actually much simpler.

The secret is that any topic can be a winner but it all depends on your approach. If you spend the time to analyze your subject and can convey with words that quality of thought that is unique to you, you'll have a powerful essay. It doesn't have to be beautifully written or crafted as the next great American novel. At its core the essay is not a "writing test." It's a "thinking test." So you do need to spend the time to make sure that your thoughts are conveyed correctly on paper. It may not be pretty writing but it has to be clear.

So how do you do this? While we can give you tips and pointers (which is what you'll read in the analysis section following every essay) the best method is to learn by example. You need to see what a successful end product looks like. While there is no single way to produce a winning essay, as you will read, there are some traits that successful essays share. You'll learn what these are by reading the examples in this book as well as the interviews with admissions officers. Then you can write a successful essay that is based on your own unique experiences, world view, way of thinking and personal style.

Why are admissions essays so important to getting into Stanford? At their most basic level, essays help admissions officers to understand who you are. While grades, test scores and academic performance can give the admissions officers an estimate on how prepared you are to handle the academic rigors of college, the essay offers the only way they can judge how your background, talents, experience and personal strengths come together to make you the best candidate for their school. For you, the applicant, the admissions essays offer the best opportunity to share who you are beyond the dry stats of your academic record. It's kind of amazing actually. You start with a blank sheet of paper and through careful selection, analysis and writing, you create a picture of yourself that impresses the admissions officers and makes them want to have you attend their school.

Ultimately, this book is designed to help you create a successful essay that gets you accepted. It will guide you toward writing that essay by sharing with you the successes of others who have written to gain admission to Stanford.

If you're like most students, you would like to know the magic formula for writing an admissions essay. Although we would love to be able to tell you, unfortunately, no such formula exists. Writing is so individual and the options so limitless, that it's impossible to develop a combination that will work for *every* essay. However, this doesn't mean that we're going to send you off with laptop in hand, without some guidance. Throughout this book you are going to see the "right way" to do things. So we thought it would be useful to start off with a few common mistakes that other students have made. You'll want to avoid these. In fact, some of these mistakes are so bad that they will almost guarantee that your essay will fail. So avoid these at all costs!

1. **Trying to be someone else.** This may sound very obvious, and well, it is. But you'd be surprised at how many students don't heed this simple piece of advice. A lot of students think that they need to be who the admissions officers want them to be; but, in reality, the admissions officers want you to be you. They aren't looking for the perfect student who is committed to every subject area, volunteers wholeheartedly for every cause, plays multiple sports with aptitude and has no faults. Instead, they want to learn about the true you. Present yourself in an honest way, and you will find it much easier to write an essay about your genuine thoughts and feelings.

2. **Choosing a topic that sounds good but that you don't care about.** Many students think that colleges seek students who have performed a lot of community service, and it is true that colleges value contributions to your community. However, this doesn't mean that you must write about community service, especially when it's not something that has played a major role for you. The same holds true for any other topic. It's critical that you select a topic that's meaningful to you because you will be able to write about the topic in a complete and personal way.

3. **Not thinking before writing.** You should spend as much time thinking about what you will write as actually putting words on paper. This will help you weed out the topics that just don't go anywhere, determine which topic has the greatest pull for you and figure out exactly what you want to say. It can help to talk yourself through your essay aloud or discuss your thoughts with

a parent, teacher or friend. The other person may see an angle or a flaw that you do not.

4. **Not answering the question.** While this seems simple enough, many students simply do not heed this. The advice is especially pertinent for those who recycle essays. We highly recommend recycling because it saves you time to write one essay that you use for many colleges, but the caveat is that you need to edit the essay so that it answers the question being asked. It turns admissions officers off when students submit an essay, even a well-written one, that doesn't answer the question. They think that the students either aren't serious enough about the college to submit an essay that has been specifically written or at least edited for that college, or that they just don't follow directions. Either way, that's not the impression you want to give.

5. **Not sharing something about yourself.** As you know, the main purpose of the admissions essay is to impart something about yourself that's not found in the application. Still, many students forget this, especially when writing about a topic such as a person they'd like to meet or a favorite book or piece of literature. In these cases, they may write so much about why they admire the person or the plot of the book that they forget to show the connection to themselves. Always ask yourself if you are letting the admissions officers know something about yourself through your essay.

6. **Forgetting who your readers are.** Naturally you speak differently to your friends than your teachers, and when it comes to the essay, some applicants essentially address the admissions officers with a too-friendly high five instead of a handshake. In other words, it's important to be yourself in the essay, but you should remember that the admissions officers are adults not peers. The essay should be comfortable but not too informal. Remember that adults generally have a more conservative view of what's funny and what's appropriate. At the same time, admissions officers are generally not senior citizens. They are typically younger, sometimes recent college graduates, and more in tune with teenage interests and popular culture than you may think. The best

way to make sure you're hitting the right tone is to ask an adult to read your essay and give you feedback.

7. **Tackling too much of your life.** Because the essay offers a few hundred words to write about an aspect of your life, some students think that they need to cram in as many aspects of their life as possible. This is not the approach we recommend. An essay of 500 to 800 words doesn't afford you the space to write about your 10 greatest accomplishments since birth or about everything that you did during your three-week summer program in Europe. Rather, the space can probably fit one or two accomplishments or one or two experiences from the summer program. Instead of trying to share your whole life, share what we call a slice of your life. By doing so, you will give your essay focus and you will have the space to cover the topic in greater depth.

8. **Having a boring introduction.** Students have started their essays by repeating the question asked and even stating their names. This does little to grab the attention of the admissions officers. Sure, they'll read the whole essay, but it always helps to have a good start. Think about how you can describe a situation that you were in, convey something that you strongly believe in or share an anecdote that might not be expected. An introduction won't make or break your essay, but it can start you off in the right direction.

9. **Latching on to an issue that you don't really care about.** One of the prompts for the Common Application is, "Discuss some issue of personal, local, national, or international concern and its importance to you." The key to answering this question is to carefully think about these words: "its importance to you." This is what students most often overlook. They select an issue and write about the issue itself, but they don't really explain why it is important to them or how they see themselves making an impact. If you write about an issue, be sure to pick one that is truly meaningful to you and that you know something about. You'll probably score extra kudos if you can describe how you have done something related to the issue.

10. **Resorting to gimmicks.** Applicants have been known to enclose a shoe with their essays along with a note that reads, "Now I have one foot in the door." They have also printed their essays in different fonts and colors, sent gifts or food and even included mood music that's meant to set the mood while the admissions officer reads the essay. A few students have even sent cash! While gimmicks like this may grab some attention, they don't do much to further the applicants, especially those few who've sent money, a definite no-no. It's true that you want for your essay to stand out but not in a way in which the admissions officer thinks that you are inappropriate or just plain silly. If you have an idea for something creative, run it by a teacher or counselor to see what he or she thinks first.

11. **Trying to make too many points.** It's better to have a single, well thought-out message in your essay than many incomplete ones. Focusing allows you to go into depth into a specific topic and make a strong case for your position. Write persuasively. You can use examples to illustrate your point.

12. **Not being specific.** If you think about some of the best stories you've been told, the ones that you remember the most are probably filled with details. The storyteller may have conveyed what he or she thought, felt, heard or saw. From the information imparted, you may have felt like you were there or you may have developed a mental image of the situation. This is precisely the experience that you would like the admissions officers to have when reading your essay. The key to being memorable is providing as many details as possible. What thoughts were going through your mind? What did you see or hear? What were you feeling during the time? Details help bring the admissions officers into your mind to feel your story.

13. **Crossing the line.** Some students take to heart the advice to share something about themselves, but they end up sharing too much. They think that they must be so revealing that they use their essay to admit to something that they would never have confessed otherwise. There have been students who have written about getting drunk, feeling suicidal or pulling pranks on their teachers. It's possible that in the right context, these topics might

work. For example, if the pranks were lighthearted and their teachers had a good sense of humor about them, that's acceptable. But for the most part, these kinds of topics are highly risky. The best way to determine if you've crossed the line is to share your idea with a couple of adults and get their reactions.

14. **Repeating what's in the application form.** The essay is not the application form, and it is not a resume. In other words, the essay is the best opportunity that you'll have to either delve into something you wrote in the application form or to expound on something new that doesn't really fit on the application form. It doesn't help you to regurgitate what's already on the application form.

15. **Not having a connection with the application form.** While you don't want to repeat information from the application form verbatim in your essay, it's usually a good idea to have some continuity between the form and your essay. If you write an essay about how your greatest passion in life is playing the piano and how you spend 10 hours a week practicing, this hobby should be mentioned in the application form along with any performances you've given or awards you've won. It doesn't make sense to write about how you love an activity in the essay and then to have no mention of it in the application form. Remember that the admissions officers are looking at your application in its entirety, and they should have a complete and cohesive image of you through all the pieces, which include the application form, essay, transcript, recommendations and interview.

16. **Not going deep enough.** One of the best pieces of advice that we give students is to keep asking, "Why?" As an example, let's say that you are writing an essay on organizing a canned food drive. Ask yourself why you wanted to do this. Your answer is that you wanted to help the homeless. Ask yourself why this was important to you. Your answer is that you imagined your family in this situation. You would greatly appreciate if others showed compassion and helped you. Why else? Because you wanted to gain hands-on experience as a leader. The point of this exercise is to realize that it's not enough to just state the facts or tell what happened, that you organized a canned food drive. What makes

an essay truly compelling is explaining the "why." You want the readers of your essay to understand your motivation. Keep asking yourself why until you have analyzed the situation as fully as possible. The answers you come up with are what will make your essay stronger.

17. **Not getting any feedback.** Practically every article that you read in a magazine, book or newspaper or on the Internet has been edited. The reason is that writing should not be an isolated experience. You may know exactly what you want to convey in your own mind, but when you put it on paper, it may not come out as clearly as it was in your mind. It helps to get feedback. Ask parents, teachers or even friends to read and comment on your essay. They can help you identify what can be edited out, what needs to be explained better or how you can improve your work.

18. **Getting too much feedback.** Asking one or two people for feedback on your essay is probably enough. If you ask more than that, you may lose the focus of your writing. Having too many editors dilutes your work because everyone has a different opinion. If you try to incorporate all of the opinions, your essay will no longer sound like you.

19. **Trying to be extraordinarily different.** There are some people who are extraordinarily different, but the truth is that most of us aren't. What's more important than conveying yourself as the most unique person at your school is that you demonstrate self-analysis, growth or insight.

20. **Ruling out common topics.** There are topics that admissions officers see over and over again such as your identity, your relationship with your family, extracurricular activities and the Big Game. While these topics are very common, it doesn't mean that you shouldn't write about them. Your topic is not as important as what you say about it. For example, many students choose to write about their moms or dads. A parent can be one of the most influential persons in a student's life, and it makes sense that this would be the topic of many students' essays. So don't rule out Mom or Dad, but do rule out writing about Mom or Dad in the way that every other person will write. Explain how your dad

made banana pancakes every morning and what that taught you about family, or how your mom almost got into a fight with another mom who made a racist comment. Make a common topic uncommon by personalizing it.

21. **Forcing humor.** You've probably seen at least one sitcom on TV or one monologue by Jimmy Kimmel or Stephen Colbert with a joke that fell flat. Maybe you groaned at the TV or gave it an un-amused expression. Keep in mind that the jokes on TV are written by professional writers who earn large salaries to be funny. Now, remember that the great majority of us are not headed down this career path. What this means is that you shouldn't force humor into your essay. If you're a funny writer, then by all means, inject some humor. Just be sure to ask an adult or two to read the essay to see if they agree with you that it is funny. If you're not humorous, then it's okay. You don't need to force it.

22. **Writing the essay the night before it's due.** Almost every student has done it—waited until the last minute to write a paper or do a project. Sometimes it comes out all right, but sometimes not so much. It is not wise to procrastinate when it comes to writing a college admissions essay. It takes time. Even if you are able to write an essay the night before it's due, it's still better not to. The best essays marinate. Their authors write, take some time away from it and then return to it later with a fresh mind.

23. **Failing the thumb test.** As you are writing your essay, place your thumb over your name. Could you put another name at the top because it could be an essay written by many other students? Or is the essay personal to you so that basically yours is the only name that could be at the top? If you fail the thumb test, it's time to rethink the topic or your approach to it. You want your essay to be unique to *you*.

24. **Forgetting to proofread.** Some students put the wrong college name in their essays, a mistake that could easily be avoided by proofreading. Many more students have spelling, grammatical or punctuation errors. While these types of errors usually aren't completely detrimental, they can be distracting at best and be signs to the admissions officers that you're careless and not

serious about their college at worst. Avoid this by not only using your computer's spell check but by asking someone else to help proofread your essay. Twice is better.

25. **Not writing to the specific college.** In addition to learning about you, the admissions officers also hope to learn how you would fit in at Stanford. You don't need to explicitly list reasons why Stanford is the best place for you, but it helps to keep in the back of your mind that Stanford is seeking students who demonstrate "intellectual vitality," who are thoughtful and reflective and who have a passion for learning that extends beyond class assignments.

26. **Not spending time on the rest of your application.** Remember that the essay is one piece of the application. It can certainly help your chances of being accepted, but you need to have everything else in place as well. Sure, it takes time to work on the application form, recommendation letters and interviews, but you are taking actions now that will affect the next four years of your life and beyond. It's worth the effort.

How to Use This Book

Now that you have a clear of idea of the mistakes to avoid in your essay, it's time to get some advice on what you *should do*. Let's go directly to the source—Stanford admissions officers. In the next chapter, former Stanford admissions officers share what they seek in applicants and give you tips on how to make the strongest impression on them.

Then, see what makes a solid essay through the essays themselves. Of course, the point is not to copy these essays. It's to gain inspiration. It's to see what's worked in the past and to get your creativity flowing so that you can formulate in your mind how you can best approach your topic.

We've analyzed each of the essays too. You'll see that even essays written by students accepted at one of the premier colleges in the country are not perfect and have room for improvement. You'll also see the strengths of the essays so that you can make sure to incorporate similar characteristics.

By learning through example, you can create the most compelling and persuasive essay possible. You'll know what not to do, you'll with you." Stanford wants a diverse community with conversations of all kinds, but they want you to show that you're tolerant and curious.

Q: **What specific advice do you have for the third Stanford prompt?**

What matters to you, and why?

A: There's a program at Stanford run by the Office for Religious Life called, "What Matters to Me and Why." Someone gives a talk on what matters to him or her, and a discussion follows. It's meant to encourage people to get reflective. This question replaced a previous question about why you want to go to Stanford.

The answer can be anything: birdwatching, baseball or ballet. It doesn't have to be about the meaning of life, but it can be if this is something you think about. It should not be the same answer that you have for the intellectual vitality question, or your activity question on the Common Application. You should pick a topic that alongside your other answers will merge to create a portrait of a complete and interesting person. A good way to rephrase this question might be: What makes you an interesting person whom other students will want to know?

Q: **What are some of the most common mistakes that students make when writing their essays?**

A: Aside from the obvious mechanical and grammatical errors, the biggest problem applicants make is failing to individualize themselves. They tend to write what I call "first date" essays. What do you do on a first date? You avoid anything controversial, you shower beforehand and your hair is in the right place. Kids laugh at that because they don't date much these days. But they get the idea: you can be so careful that you lose the attention of your reader.

Another major mistake applicants make is not understanding what colleges want. They don't know how to "present" themselves. I abhor all language that smacks of marketing yourself, but you have to remember that colleges are fundamentally academic places. That's one of the reasons why Stanford developed the question about intellectual vitality. How many kids see themselves as intellectual? As having an idea? Very few. They don't know how to express that they're interested in something. They don't know how to reflect on themselves. A lot of this is failure of self-inquiry, failure of self-understanding. They know they need to go deep, but they're afraid because they might be vulnerable.

One of the other mistakes is when they write about a significant person. They write about *Dead Poets Society*, an amazing teacher or a grandfather. The essay becomes about that person rather than about themselves. The new prompts on the Common Application don't lead to this choice as easily as the old ones did, but it is still an easy trap to fall into.

Also, they shouldn't write about the same thing everywhere. Reading an application is like assembling a jigsaw puzzle. Only when the pieces click in does it become coherent. Each piece by itself is not that valuable.

Q: Can you think of an example of when an applicant wrote about an ordinary topic in an extraordinary way?

A: Kids think they have to write about something exceptional. You don't have to talk about climbing Half Dome in the dark with your hands handcuffed. Most of what you've lived is normal. There are kids who have very extraordinary stories. However, I've seen wonderful essays about normal life. One applicant had a summer job at a resort near Tahoe as a lifeguard. That's like watching the corn grow—nothing happens. She wrote about her need for alertness. The actual essay was about how her mind worked while nothing was happening. She is at Stanford.

Another of my students wrote about a children's book and what it was like to be four years old. It was superficial. I said, "Go back and dig deeper." She found something in her life. Her father had had a stroke, and while he recovered, his personality changed. She wrote about the difference in his manner and what that meant to her. It was very honest and touching.

Q: Are there any topics or approaches to topics that students shouldn't write about?

A: Sex is a dangerous topic because it's hard to treat it maturely. I've read some powerful essays about rape and molestation. It raises all kinds of flags to the reader that the student doesn't know what's appropriate. At Stanford, a very good student wrote about being date raped. She wrote about it tastefully but vividly. She described his hands on her body. It had originally been written for an English class. I thought it was very powerful. The Dean thought it was too graphic, and he wouldn't support her understand what the admissions officers want and, perhaps most importantly, you'll be inspired to write your own successful Stanford admissions essay.

2

STANFORD ADMISSIONS OFFICER Q&A

JON REIDER
Former Senior Associate Director of Admission at Stanford
Co-author of *Admission Matters*

Q: What specific advice do you have for the first Stanford prompt?

Stanford students possess an intellectual vitality. Reflect on an idea or experience that has been important to your intellectual development.

A: This question was designed to attract—I hate to use the word because it's overused, students passionate about ideas. As an example, let's say you are taking U.S. history. What happens if you get fascinated by the Battle of Gettysburg? You say to the teacher, "I know we don't have time to spend on this in class, but how can I learn more about it?" Another example is the kid who stays up at night thinking about a 90 degree angle. How do you bisect an angle? You can't trisect an angle, but suppose you don't believe that, and you want to prove it. You're the kind of kid who wants to learn and who stays after class to learn.

Stanford is very into the idea of the student as an entrepreneur, that you are responsible for your own educational experience. You knock on professors' doors, and you raise your hand in class. You want to demonstrate that you're the kind of student that the faculty wants to teach.

I think the right way to answer this question is to write about how you've taken responsibility for your own education. The subject doesn't matter; it could be computers or Jane Austen. What's important is that you've pursued a topic beyond what the teacher has asked you to do.

Be conscious that the person reading your essay may be less knowledgeable about the subject than you are, particularly if it's a technical topic. The typical admissions officer is usually a liberal arts major. Remember that you're writing to an intelligent layperson.

Q: What specific advice do you have for the second Stanford prompt?

Virtually all of Stanford's undergraduates live on campus. Write a note to your future roommate that reveals something about you or that will help your roommate—and us—know you better.

A: A mistake that students often make is listing all of their quirky likes and dislikes. For example, "I like Thai food. I look forward to running at the Dish, etc." I think that this essay is done best when it is on one topic rather than a whole bunch of topics.

I remember one essay where an applicant wrote about playing the piano. I can't tell you how many essays I've read about playing the piano. This kid wrote about the difference in his mind between playing a piano for an audience versus playing for himself. The essay wasn't about Beethoven or actually playing the piano but about his own mind. This kid was a thinker. It's a very mundane topic, which could kill 99 out of 100 essays, but he made it work for him.

I remember a roommate essay that showed why it's dangerous to write about religion if you are not open-minded. Stanford (and any other college) doesn't mind if you're very religious, but this student wrote, "Hi, I see that you already have a Bible, but I replaced your Bible with my Bible because mine is the true word of God. I look forward to praying with you." Stanford wants a diverse community with conversations of all kinds, but they want you to show that you're tolerant and curious.

Q: What specific advice do you have for the third Stanford prompt?

What matters to you, and why?

A: There's a program at Stanford run by the Office for Religious Life called, "What Matters to Me and Why." Someone gives a talk on what matters to him or her, and a discussion follows. It's meant to encourage people to get reflective. This question replaced a previous question about why you want to go to Stanford.

The answer can be anything: birdwatching, baseball or ballet. It doesn't have to be about the meaning of life, but it can be if this is something you think about. It should not be the same answer that you have for the intellectual vitality question, or your activity question on the Common Application. You should pick a topic that alongside your other answers will merge to create a portrait of a complete and interesting person. A good way to rephrase this question might be: What makes you an interesting person whom other students will want to know?

Q: What are some of the most common mistakes that students make when writing their essays?

A: Aside from the obvious mechanical and grammatical errors, the biggest problem applicants make is failing to individualize themselves. They tend to write what I call "first date" essays. What do you do on a first date? You avoid anything controversial, you shower beforehand and your hair is in the right place. Kids laugh at that because they don't date much these days. But they get the idea: you can be so careful that you lose the attention of your reader.

Another major mistake applicants make is not understanding what colleges want. They don't know how to "present" themselves. I abhor all language that smacks of marketing yourself, but you have to remember that colleges are fundamentally academic places. That's one of the reasons why Stanford developed the question about intellectual vitality. How many kids see themselves as intellectual? As having an idea? Very few. They don't know how to express that they're interested in something. They don't know how to reflect on themselves. A lot of this is failure of self-inquiry, failure of self-understanding. They know they need to go deep, but they're afraid because they might be vulnerable.

One of the other mistakes is when they write about a significant person. They write about *Dead Poets Society*, an amazing teacher or a grandfather. The essay becomes about that person rather than about themselves. The new prompts on the Common Application don't lead to this choice as easily as the old ones did, but it is still an easy trap to fall into.

Also, they shouldn't write about the same thing everywhere. Reading an application is like assembling a jigsaw puzzle. Only when the pieces click in does it become coherent. Each piece by itself is not that valuable.

Q: Can you think of an example of when an applicant wrote about an ordinary topic in an extraordinary way?

A: Kids think they have to write about something exceptional. You don't have to talk about climbing Half Dome in the dark with your hands handcuffed. Most of what you've lived is normal. There are kids who have very extraordinary stories. However, I've seen wonderful essays about normal life. One applicant had a summer job at a resort near Tahoe as a lifeguard. That's like watching the corn grow—nothing happens. She wrote about her need for alertness. The actual essay was about how her mind worked while nothing was happening. She is at Stanford.

Another of my students wrote about a children's book and what it was like to be four years old. It was superficial. I said, "Go back and dig deeper." She found something in her life. Her father had had a stroke, and while he recovered, his personality changed. She wrote about the difference in his manner and what that meant to her. It was very honest and touching.

Q: Are there any topics or approaches to topics that students shouldn't write about?

A: Sex is a dangerous topic because it's hard to treat it maturely. I've read some powerful essays about rape and molestation. It raises all kinds of flags to the reader that the student doesn't know what's appropriate. At Stanford, a very good student wrote about being date raped. She wrote about it tastefully but vividly. She described his hands on her body. It had originally been written for an English class. I thought it was very powerful. The Dean thought it was too graphic, and he wouldn't support her admission. I apologized to the guidance counselor. The guidance counselor told me the student was admitted to lots of colleges but not in any predictable pattern. It depended on who had read the essay.

In another case, a straight-A student wrote about being a perfectionist and how he got really upset after he had a small auto accident. He revealed a vulnerability, but the college said they thought he might implode in their high-pressure atmosphere. I knew that was unlikely since I knew the whole student, but the Dean was not persuaded. The essay was honest, but it exaggerated a trait. There's a middle ground. You want to tell the truth but not make yourself look bad in the process. This is tricky.

It can be very dangerous to write about mental health issues or anorexia, which are big problems in our society. Sometimes you have to write about a health issue because your grades dropped. Chronic fatigue, diabetes or learning disabilities are okay to write about. However, the colleges see anorexia as a flag. One college admission dean said that an applicant was very well connected at the college but was anorexic. He hesitated to admit the student because he said, "This is a big problem at our campus, and we use a lot of resources caring for these kids." I said, "You're already admitting 50 other kids with this problem, but you don't know which ones. In this case, you do." The student was admitted, but they kept an eye on her.

Another flag is kids unconsciously describing their privilege, writing about an expensive trip they went on that their parents paid for. Certain sports like horseback riding can be flags. I have a student who flew all over the country to competitions with her horse. The average admissions officer is not rich. It's not a profession you go into to make a lot of money. It is not bad to have money. It can be wonderful, in fact, but it doesn't look good to take it for granted.

The key issue is insight. What have you learned? How are you a different person? What have you gained from this experience? How have you changed during high school?

Q: How important is the essay? In your experience, has it ever made the difference between a student being accepted or not?

A: In the earlier example of the date rape essay, the kid was admissible, but the essay kept her out. However, in other cases an essay is powerful, charming and revealing, and you say this is a really good person.

It doesn't single-handedly get you in. There are literally thousands of kids with excellent credentials, high test scores, all the APs and extra-curricular activities. They're very hard to distinguish. Why is a kid with a 730 better than a kid with 710? It wasn't their formal numbers, the quantitative elements. We called it the self-presentation. The total self-presentation, all the essays, could make a difference when the numbers were high, but not definitive. But the numbers are already set; in October of your senior year, you can't do much about them. So, at that point, the essays are the one factor still in your control, plus you can actually learn something about yourself from them.

Q: Is there anything that a student might find surprising either about your selection process or about what you are looking for in the essays?

Positive things:

I want to see that you're thoughtful. I used to give a talk on writing essays. The acronym was: CHICAV-OOOP-LI. These are the traits that good essays should have:

- **C: Coherent.** You don't want to babble, and you want to have structure. The essay needs to have a theme.

- **H: Honest.** Don't just tell the truth, but be honest about yourself.

- **I: Individualized.** How do you know something you are saying is about you and you alone? It's not in the piano or lacrosse team. It's in your mind. How do you differentiate how you think from everyone else?

- **C: Concise.** The admissions officers don't want to read too much. They're reading thousands of essays. The Common Application now has a formal limit, as do the Stanford supplements. Give the reader a break.

- **A: Accurate.** Don't say Dostoyevsky wrote *War and Peace*. Spell Nietzsche's name correctly. I once read an essay with his name spelled four different ways.

- **V: Vivid.** Give vivid, concrete examples. People want stories.

Negative things:

O: Obscure. Don't be obscure. If you say you won the Rachel Austin Award at Palo Alto High School, the admissions officer may ask, what's the Rachel Austin Award? Explain it.

O: Don't be obnoxious. Remember my example of the kid who replaced her roommate's Bible.

O: Do not be obscene. Don't be too graphic.

P: Don't plagiarize. In answering an essay about picking an adjective and writing about it, one girl wrote a very strong essay in which she made up her own word and defined it. Five years later, another girl copied this essay word for word and submitted it.

More positive points:

L: Likeable. What makes someone likeable? Would you like to have dinner with this person every night for a year in the dorm?

I: Interesting. This is the hardest thing of all for kids. A lot is in the eye of the beholder, the reader. A good essay is written self-consciously. You want to be aware of thinking about what will interest someone else. This means not being too safe or too conventional.

Another example is of an applicant for transfer admission. She was German, and she wrote an essay about going to high school in Sweden. She had a very difficult teacher, and she struggled through the class. Only at the end, she told you who the teacher was—it was the Swedish language. It was a brilliant essay about her own mind.

So I suggest: Imagine that you're not writing to a Stanford admissions officer, but to a Martian admissions officer. The admissions officer can scan your mind. Your essay is like a GPS to your mind, and you want them to understand your mind through the essay.

Jon Reider is the director of college counseling at San Francisco University High School and former senior associate director of admission at Stanford. He is also the co-author of *Admission Matters*.

IRENA SMITH
Former Stanford Admissions Officer

Q: Can you give students an idea of what happens to their applications and essays after they are received by the college?

A: When I worked in the admission office at Stanford, we first conducted a multitiered sort of the applications into competitive and non-competitive. Factors we looked for included GPAs and standardized test scores. If you weren't at a competitive level, it would be very likely you wouldn't be admitted unless there were huge mitigating circumstances.

Then, a reader would do a full read of the application, paying close attention to letters of recommendation, extracurricular activities, essays and the applicant's contribution to his or her school. The reader would make a recommendation and pass the application to a more senior level dean. The dean would sign off or reverse the recommendation.

Committee evaluation didn't occur until the very end, when we were reviewing minute differences among applicants. The process was mostly on paper in which you would see the comments from the person who did the initial sorting and write your own comments as a full reader. Three to four people typically reviewed every application. It was a very careful process.

Q: What specific advice do you have for the first Stanford prompt?

Stanford students possess intellectual vitality. Reflect on an idea or experience that has been important to your intellectual development.

A: This is a hard topic for some students, and the answer really depends on the student. The student should focus on the areas that he or she is truly excited about. For example, if you are interested in applied math, you can write about topics such as your calculus class or about the wonders of the abacus. Or, if philosophy is an interest, you might write about having a conversation with somebody about reading Nietzsche. The point is to think about which intellectual ideas are exciting to you.

Q: **What specific advice do you have for the second Stanford prompt?**

Virtually all of Stanford's undergraduates live on campus. Write a note to your future roommate that reveals something about you or that will help your roommate—and us—know you better.

A: That's the fun one. It gets a lot of students to go off filter. I don't know that a roommate would want to know about a disagreeable habit. Remember that oversharing can go against a student. I would suggest thinking about if the question were reversed: What would you want to know from a future roommate? Try to be more imaginative than, "You bring the beanbag chair and I'll bring the fridge." Share a story that illustrates how you will enhance communal living in a residential environment. For example, maybe you have a skill in juggling or magic or maybe your siblings taught you how to share a living space. Think about the hobbies or abilities that you have that will help you live with a roommate.

Q: **What specific advice do you have for the third Stanford prompt?**

What matters to you, and why?

A: It's important to ground your essay in the specifics as much as possible. You might write about a family heirloom or a story about a place where something significant happened. Remember that we're hardwired to respond to concrete examples. You need to drill down into that story that only you can tell. It might be a pair of running shoes that you can't throw away or a smile you shared with a stranger—something that is honest, true and specific to you.

Q: **What are some of the most common mistakes that students make when writing their essays?**

A: I've seen two of the most common mistakes which are really on opposite ends of the same spectrum. The first is to write a generic let me tell you about my great qualities essay, using all of the buzzwords— leadership, perseverance, motivation, etc. It's safe to say, "I'm a strong leader" or "I never quit in the face of adversity," but it's also nondescript and generic. Here is where show, don't tell really holds true. It's much more impressive to show how you shepherded twelve five-year-olds to the pool at 8 a.m. rather than say, "I'm a great leader."

The second mistake is oversharing—there are things that you shouldn't share with an admissions officer. Examples I saw at Stanford include taking a health problem that is not life-threatening like eczema or lactose intolerance and writing about it with a great deal of pathos. Having a debilitating disease is one thing, but taking a Lactaid before eating ice cream is another.

Q: Can you think of an example of when an applicant wrote about an ordinary topic in an extraordinary way?

A: Students sometimes write in really extraordinary ways about their families. They start digging and find great material. One student wrote about how her extended family celebrated Christmas with the same traditions each year. On her 16th birthday she announced that she wasn't going to participate in the celebration any more. In her essay, she described the family's shocked silence and everyone's reactions.

Another student wrote about a Persian custom which is best described as excessive politeness or hospitality. For example, if I said I like your coat or shoes, you would be obligated to take them off and offer them to me. The student wrote that she would occasionally lose her dessert that way, because of this custom. It's not earth-shattering, but it's interesting and true to her experience.

All too often students feel like if they haven't scaled Mt. Everest with their pet goat while blogging about it, they have nothing to say. Try to dig a little deeper into your everyday experiences, even if they seem ordinary, and try to find the extraordinary in them.

Q: Are there any topics or approaches to topics that students shouldn't write about?

A: Gloating essays about high school pranks should be avoided. Writing about how you're a juggler and can juggle seven balls is fine. Writing about how you drove a car into the school pool or glued all the locks shut at your school is not. In the right context, some pranks can be funny but not in the admissions essay. This shows a lack of judgment. You don't want the reader to ask if you would be a good citizen or a goofball on campus.

Q: How important is the essay? In your experience, has it ever made the difference between a student being accepted or not?

A: I don't want students to freak out and think everything is riding on this. Typically the essay is one of many pieces, and a college will not accept or reject you based on the essay. In rare cases in which a student says something hateful or objectionable or puts no effort into the essay, it can cause the student to be rejected, but it's extremely rare to have an essay that's the fatal flaw.

Will a marginal student get in because of an essay alone? Probably not. In an ideal test situation if you have 10 applicants and they're all the same and one of the essays shines, that can tip the student into the yes pile. In the end, the student will never really know. What's more important is to devote the time to write your best story where you can say, 'I couldn't have done any better.'

Q: Is there anything that a student might find surprising either about the selection process or about what you are looking for in the essays?

A: As a general rule, admissions officers are not looking for any particular thing. They're looking to be engaged or surprised. They aren't looking for magic words like leadership, tenacity or adversity. There is no topic that if you write about it, you're in.

Students might be surprised by how open-minded admissions officer are and how informal you are tacitly encouraged to be. Admissions officers read 10 to 30 applications a day. They want to be engaged. They don't mind if you use contractions or make cultural references. There's a degree of informality that goes along with being open about yourself.

Also, contrary to popular belief, admissions officers are not a bunch of mean old people. High school seniors have this image of admissions officers as grammar Nazi English professors with suede patches on their elbows waiting to pounce on them. In reality, they tend to skew pretty young, typically under 40 because as they get older they might become high school counselors or move into more senior positions. They tend to be hip and very enamored with the high school student demographic. They're a friendly audience.

Before starting their essays, a lot of students read books of college essays by admitted students, but they read them without context. They don't know how many drafts the essay has been through. All they know is that the student has been accepted to a particular college. In my opinion, it's much better to read creative, first person non-fiction, which can be really fun and which removes students from those who are applying to college. David Sedaris and Mindy Kaling have interesting things to say about themselves in the first person that have nothing to do with leadership or tenacity but everything to do with humor and imagination and a particular way of looking at the world. Reading first person non-fiction gives students a good sense of how to speak about themselves.

Irena Smith, Ph.D., is a former Stanford admissions officer, a writer and editor, and a private college admissions counselor in the San Francisco Bay Area.

3

ACADEMIC PASSION

"Linda"

Jimmy Chen

TO ANY OUTSIDE OBSERVER, SHE WAS far from perfect. Linda was bulky, inefficient, and jerky, nothing like the other slim, flawless models. But we could not have been more proud of her.

Even though Linda, the catapult that my friend and I built for Science Olympiad, did not win any official awards at Regionals, we were still satisfied to carry her triumphantly from the competition. Scrambling to cover all of the events, our Science Olympiad team realized the week before the competition that we had nobody competing in "Storm the Castle," the catapult-building event. That is why several of my friends and I found ourselves in a garage at 2:00 a.m. on a Friday night, sawing and sanding, drilling and calculating.

The real fruit of our labor was not a clumsy piece of woodwork that flung tennis balls across the yard; it was a deeper understanding of science and practicality (I suppose this episode should also have taught a lesson about procrastination, but that has proven itself a truly difficult lesson to teach). Perhaps because my experience with science has been largely limited to the classroom, I was sheepishly surprised to discover that the physics equations from my textbooks actually applied to the workings of the real world. $T = f * x$ wasn't just some didactic invention created to make physics tests more difficult; it meant that a longer lever arm would yield greater torque, and thus a longer throw.

The way that science is taught in schools tends to construct these artificial walls where, as far as our classes are concerned, each topic is segregated. Both literally and figuratively, Linda transcended these walls. In one not-so-fluid motion, she proved to our notes and calculators that rotational force and bidimensional kinematics were in fact long lost brothers, not distant strangers divided in the textbook by eighty-seven pages of insulation. By analogy I realized that what I learned in chemistry still applied in the biology classroom down the hall. Perhaps the reason that this realization, which seems so completely basic, seemed so amazing to me was that it had simply never resonated in this fashion before. I had always considered science the ugly stepsister of higher-level math, which seemed the epitome of impracticability. Up until that night in the garage, these interdisciplinary relationships appeared nothing more than a popular rumor. My discovery of the contrary provided a fresh set of lenses with which to view the art of science as a practical yet dynamic field, whether it appears in tepid textbooks, during lengthy lectures, or in dusty garages.

When we carried Linda to the State Science Olympiad competition, it was with only a few minor tweaks and the same sense of ridiculous pride. The tennis ball that had once flown across the garage now flew across the driveway. The night before the competition, still impressed with the novelty of having a catapult at our disposal, we amused ourselves by flinging balls of crumpled up paper (or a bouncy ball, a golf ball, a shoe) off of our hotel's second-story balcony. The annoyed protests of the other members of our Science Olympiad team below proved that our new perspective of science was already paying quick dividends. Linda was part of the family.

ANALYSIS

Jimmy's essay is a simply structured narrative, but its simplicity in structure makes it all the more impressive in that it manages to communicate Jimmy's personality and voice, current activities and interests, and even his potential future interests in such a straightforward story.

Jimmy begins by introducing his sense of humor as he introduces Linda: Jimmy intentionally misdirects his readers at the start of the essay when he describes Linda, who in all respects seems to be a woman. Jimmy takes a risk with his frank assessment of Linda's physical attributes and clumsiness, which might be alarming if it were actually about a woman, but he renders it endearing when he mentions his team's pride in her, and he reveals a quirky but smart sense of humor and a deft mastery of comic writing when he casually makes apparent in the next paragraph that Linda is actually a catapult.

Jimmy's sense of humor and his overall conversational tone throughout the essay make him seem personable, genuine, humble and honest: he reveals weaknesses, such as the clumsiness of his team's hastily built catapult or the sheepishness with which he reacts to seeing physics equations in action, and biases, against science, "the ugly stepsister of higher-level math, which seemed the epitome of impracticability." Without these admissions, Jimmy's bait-and-switch trick at the opening of the essay, in which he describes Linda as if she were a woman, and his mention of flinging objects at other Science Olympiad teams from his hotel balcony, might read as brash and rude, but tempered by Jimmy's honesty, they instead come off as endearing.

On the other hand, Jimmy's essay's strength does not merely lie in the fact that it is cleverly crafted to reveal its author's sense of humor and personality. Jimmy also communicates a strong sense of his own interests, ideas and his potential future. His very choice of subject, his team's entry into the Science Olympiad, already suggests his current interests and extracurricular involvement, and his use of specific examples illustrating his realization that abstract physics equations map onto real-life results demonstrates his facility in the subjects: "T = f * x wasn't just some didactic invention created to make physics tests more difficult; it meant that a longer lever arm would yield greater torque, and thus a longer throw."

This essay successfully showcases not only Jimmy's wit and personality, but also his interests and passions. This success is not only due to Jimmy's authentic and unique voice and casual, conversational tone, but also to the simplicity of its structure: Jimmy recounts a single, brief event, and he gives us just enough detail to understand the premises, which allows him to spend the bulk of his essay fully fleshing out the circumstances that brought about his realization, its ramifications not just for his science project but also for the way that he approaches science and math as disciplines and to include fun and humorous details and descriptions that allow us to see him as a person as well as a student.

"Music, Math and More"

Kendall Weierich

Essay prompt: An intellectually engaging idea or experience

IT'S MY GUILTY PLEASURE.

Whenever I read a book, perform a lab experiment or solve a calculus problem, I find a way to connect that subject with music. The relation of music to just about any aspect of my life drives my curiosity and helps me better understand the original subject. In English we were reading *Huckleberry Finn* and Mark Twain had just referenced a specific musical composition. I spent hours that night tracking down the song, reading about its historical origin and studying the score. Incredibly, the theme of the song fit the plot's movement to a T and even foreshadowed what was to occur!

In math, we learned about the "Golden Proportion" as it applies to calculus. I later discovered that this most aesthetically pleasing ratio, 1: .618, is not exclusively applicable to math. Have you ever wondered why, after intermission, the second "half" of a performance is shorter than the first? Or why the apexes of Bach's chorales fall in a certain part of the music? By structuring a performance according to the golden ratio, studies have shown audiences will have a much more enjoyable experience. This ratio is everywhere: in the human body, in architecture, in art, and, of course, in music.

Sometimes the connections I make are simply personal. I am synesthetic; I often associate letters and words with note pitches and chords with colors. When I play the piano, I mentally paint a picture of the song. As I write an essay for school, I can hear its melody. To me, Chopin's waltz in A-flat major expresses the conversation of French lovers, but unfortunately my thesis paper for history articulates an atonal mess.

All of these instances and more have demonstrated to me that no matter what major I choose or field of profession I enter, I can and will be able to tie it to music in some way or another. So please don't mind me humming along to the reaction of copper chloride and zinc; it's perfectly normal.

ANALYSIS

This essay is a great example of how an ordinary subject, in this case music, can be used to illustrate a student's intellectual vitality. Many high schools students would probably refer to music as a "guilty pleasure" especially in this day and age where everyone seems to be running around with a headphone in one ear. However, Kendall shows us how music has become a part of her academic life as well as her personal life. Specific examples of how she uses music to better understand math, literature and other subjects help us understand how Kendall's analytical process works.

The best example is given in the second paragraph where we see the author reading *Huckleberry Finn*. Kendall notes that when she found a song she didn't know, she "spent hours that night tracking down the song, reading about its historical origin and studying the score." The thoroughness of Kendall's research shows her passion for seeking knowledge. She was curious enough about the specific piece to not only find it, but to also understand its significance to the larger work. The fact that Kendall was willing to look all this up on her own shows both initiative and sincere interest. Furthermore, we see Kendall reason out how the music worked; she noted that aspects of the song reflected events in the book's plot. Impressive as this analysis is, it would have been even more impressive if she had given specifics what similarities she noticed between the music and the book's plot.

The essay then elaborates on how Kendall's passion for making connections between music and classwork applies to multiple subject areas. For example, Kendall then relates the structure of music to the "Golden Proportion," a math concept she learned in school. This breadth of analysis shows how Kendall is an academically well-rounded student. We then learn that this is due to synesthesia, a rare trait that causes one to perceive the world differently. This fact both helps us understand where Kendall's passion for music comes from, and it helps us understand her better as a person. Admitting to having synesthesia doesn't quite fit anywhere on a college application. Yet, by mentioning it in the essay portion of the application, we both get to know that Kendall has synesthesia, and understand what having that trait means for her academic development.

Kendall's final paragraph wraps up the essay nicely by alluding to how her passion for music, and synesthetic perspective on the world, is likely to affect her future self. She specifically notes, "no matter what major I choose [...] I can and will be able to tie it to music in some way." This is important considering that Kendall mentioned earlier that relating various subjects to music peaks her interest in those subjects. Therefore, Kendall assures the reader that regardless of what academic challenges she might face in college, she will find an interesting way to interact with the material. That is a true sign of intellectual vitality.

"The Value of an Open Mind"

Rob Resma

Essay prompt: An intellectually engaging idea or experience

SOME BELIEVE INTELLECT IS BASED ON how much knowledge you can stuff in your cerebrum; however, if the lid to the cooking pot is closed, how can you put in the ingredients? At the beginning of my freshman year my mind was sort of like a 256-bit Advanced Encryption Standard, locked shut. In other words, due to my closed mind, I had no desire to learn! It took three years of high school, but one Saturday morning at Kumon, my tutoring job, I had my epiphany which broke the encryption!

In Kumon, I adjusted to my new job quicker than the rate at which blood flows through the body. After two months of tutoring students in math and reading, while simultaneously grading piles of worksheets, I earned the privilege to work Saturday shifts with Mrs. S.

Fifteen minutes early on my first Saturday morning shift, I prepared for the oncoming flood of students. Introducing herself, Mrs. S. started a conversation with me about my life goals. I told her all about my 15 year dream career goal as an oncologist. She then said, "I hope destiny shines brightly on your future." Stopped in my tracks, I curiously asked, "You believe in destiny?" A passionate Hindu, Mrs. S. told me about the essence of dharma and destiny, a totally different view from my existentialist and Catholic mindset. I had an awakening! Instead of going home that day I took a trip to the public library and read several books about Hinduism.

Reflecting upon the talk with Mrs. S. Saturday, I realized that keeping an open mind is the key to intellectualism. If my mind were so closed to ideas, I could never appreciate the world of knowledge around me. I could spend my time forcing myself to cram data into a gigabyte motherboard, or fitting it all in a 2 terabyte external hard drive. To be an intellect is not to have perfect grades or outstanding test scores. It is to cherish the journey of learning. Because I achieved my "nirvana," my limits are undefined.

ANALYSIS

Rob takes a simple event—a non-event, really—in his life and turns it into a college essay that reveals his open mind and dedication to exploring new viewpoints. The conversation he had with Mrs. S. was relatively ordinary, but he took the extraordinary step of immediately going to the library to learn more about Hinduism. Rob follows the well-worn adage that it best to "show, not tell" by not just claiming to be open-minded, but providing an example that illustrates how open-minded he is. As you prepare to write your own essay, you might consider which of your personal qualities you want to highlight. Then, try brainstorming moments when you demonstrated each quality. As Rob's essay proves, these moments don't have to be life changing or melodramatic in order to be effective. The goal is to find a moment that epitomizes the aspect of your personality that you want admissions officers to remember.

Rob compares his mind to "a 256-bit Advanced Encryption Standard, locked shut," a simile he returns to throughout the essay. Making comparisons like this one, especially if they relate to your interests or mesh well with the theme of the essay, is one way to differentiate your piece from the piles of other essays on similar topics. Using a single metaphor throughout your essay creates a sense of cohesion and shows that, as the author, you have a firm grasp of what you're trying to say and how you want to say it. This technique works best when you avoid mixing metaphors; in Rob's case, it would have been better not to introduce the "cooking pot" comparison in addition to the computer-related similes.

Including a few lines of dialogue can also add a spark to your essay. In this piece, Mrs. S.'s wish that "destiny shines brightly on your future" is an especially nice touch, because the phrase in and of itself is poetic and memorable. If you choose to include dialogue or quotes of any sort, make sure they are juicy ones. If a quotation is not any more exciting or catchy than what you could have written in a paraphrase, then skip it.

Notice that Rob peppers his essay with facts about himself that help readers know him better, even if they aren't the main focus of the essay. For instance, he mentions how quickly he took to his tutoring job and describes his long-standing dream of becoming an oncologist. The college essay is a good opportunity to slip in details like this, as long as they don't distract from your main argument.

"Learning by Living"

Vienna Harvey

"MOMMY, THAT STRANGER'S GOING TO GET me!" With that panicked cry, my 3-year-old self effectively sealed the deal that would change my life.

My parents had been musing about homeschooling for some time. If my dad were to fulfill his dream of living on a sailboat, homeschooling would be a necessity. In the wake of the "stranger" incident, my parents decided that the homeschooling might as well start right then. My mom withdrew me from preschool.

The story about my pre-school fear of strangers has become a family favorite. The homeschooling outcome, however, was no joke. It has become a central part of my identity. For our 4 years on the sailboat, beginning when I was 8, I could learn what was relevant to me at the time. Standing atop a ruined pyramid in Tikal, the pre-Columbian king 18-Rabbit was simply more vivid than George Washington. Two years later, however, as we docked our boat at Mount Vernon, George Washington became highly interesting.

At first I had little say in my education. Homeschooling was simply a decision my parents had made for me. When we moved ashore, my parents saw no reason to stop, so we continued as homeschoolers. When I reached high school age, though, my parents left the choice up to me. Although I had many homeschooled friends who decided to attend public high school, I chose to continue homeschooling. I enjoyed the flexibility it gave me and didn't relish the idea of spending all day in a classroom.

My parents and I decided not to replicate a standard high school curriculum as some homeschooling families do. As I became more involved in my own education, this approach allowed me to discover and pursue subjects I was truly interested in. In 10th grade, I started taking classes at Old Dominion University, a short bus ride from my house. Over the next few years, classes at ODU represented an increasingly large part of my coursework.

In retrospect, I can see that many of the classes I have chosen to take share a common theme: Why do people behave the way they do? Psychology, criminology, and sociology all address this question from different perspectives. This realization could not have come from a pre-set curriculum. Now I may choose to pursue a career in the social sciences, a course of study I might never have considered had I not been homeschooled.

There are many stereotypes about homeschoolers: homeschoolers are unsocialized, homeschoolers are all Christians, homeschoolers are geeky. I fit very few of the stereotypes, yet I am still a homeschooler. Even now, when I take all but one of my classes at a university, I am still a homeschooler. When I enter college for real next fall, I will still be a homeschooler: I will be involved in and directing my own education as I have for the past several years. This is part of who I am now, something I will take with me for the rest of my life.

ANALYSIS

With a shocking opening Vienna immediately pulls the reader into her essay: What stranger? What's going on? What deal? How did her life change, and for better or worse? With the next sentence we learn that the "deal" refers to Vienna's parents' decision to home school her and the rest of the essay focuses on how her homeschooling experience became an integral part of her identity.

Instead of listing all the things she learned, Vienna uses specific subjects to support her central theme of real-life experience making education relevant. Notice how she slips novel-length adventures into her essay: she gives just enough detail to illustrate her world-ranging experiences while leaving the reader eager to talk to her in person. Tell me more about growing up on a boat! Where else did you go? What other sights did you see?

While she acknowledges her parents' role in her education, she also explains why she herself chose to continue homeschooling and her own role in and ownership of her education. Colleges and universities love to hear that students feel responsible for their own education—rather than be passive couch-potatoes—and Vienna reinforces the image of an active self-learning by discussing the university courses she chose as part of her "home schooling." Without saying it directly, Vienna *shows* that not only is she ready for university, but that she's already successfully accomplished quite a bit of college-level coursework, thus putting to rest any apprehension the school might have about the quality of her home schooling or her ability to "adjust" to the rigors of the higher education curriculum.

The main weakness in Vienna's essay as a whole is the same strength with which it began: it raises too many questions but provides few answers, especially when those answers could have been used to "flesh out" her portrait. She said she "enjoyed the flexibility [home schooling] gave me and didn't relish the idea of spending all day in a classroom": what did she use that flexibility for, and what aspect of the classroom instruction turned her off? She's identified a main line of inquiry in her studies—Why do people behave the way they do?—but why does that interest her? Is she still scarred by the stranger incident? Does it stem from her world-wide travels? Is she so anti-social that people present themselves to her as an alien species fit for analysis? And why could this realization not have come from a "pre-set curriculum"? A statement like that, given without support, could give the reader the idea that she's employing stereotypes herself, and while she addresses stereotypes of homeschoolers and says she fits "very few" of them, which ones does she fit? And how are they a positive part of her identity?

Remember to take every opportunity to reveal another aspect of you: many other people will be writing about similar "unique" life experiences and up-bringings, so what will set you apart is the personality that shines through your written portrait.

"Intellectual Interest"

Ellora Karmarkar

Essay prompt: An intellectually engaging idea or experience

WHILE SITTING IN MY UNCLE'S LAB, I looked at a slide collection of living lung cells that resembled a translucent cobblestone road. When a cell was injected with calcium, a signal tracked by a pathway of blue light traveled throughout the system. As my uncle explained the process, my visualizations of the terms he used flashed through my mind: "anemone-like G protein receptors embedded in cytoplasm, reaching out with their feathery arms. Ligands binding to the receptors by their curly tails, like sea dragons. Spiky tyrosine kinase receptors, awaiting the next signal."

The idea that cells speak to each other through chemicals has always fascinated me. There was so much that I didn't know. What did these receptors really look like? How were they sending these messages? Seeing a tangible image on the screen stimulated multiple questions I had already wondered about. "If my lung cells communicate like this, how do my neurons speak to each other? What is physically happening in my brain while I think about this?" I smiled as I realized that all of the folding proteins and firing neurons that I had loved learning about in biology had tremendous, mysterious roles to play; not only in our fundamental mechanisms of life, but in our behavior. My uncle, who thought that I was asleep by then, was shocked when he looked up and saw me leaning, enraptured, toward the screen.

ANALYSIS

There's not a lot in terms of plot or narrative, but that's clearly not the point of this essay—Ellora's goal here is to communicate what it is about cell biology she finds so intriguing, and she doesn't need an anecdote to accomplish that. She instead gives the essay some simple background—sitting in her uncle's lab, looking at slide images of cells—and focuses instead on sharing her completely overwhelming fascination with biology as well as communicating her unique way of visualizing it and showcasing her descriptive ability.

Ellora elects to illustrate not just a subject or a topic that interests her, but rather, a specific aspect of a topic that interests her, which allows her to be very specific without need for much introductory material—crucial in these shorter essays. She chooses to illustrate how fascinating it is not just to think about cell pathways and signal receptors, but how she is able to visualize it, and how that vivid, creative visualization has further fueled her interest in biology. Ellora's wonderfully colorful, dynamic, Alice-in-Wonderland-esque visualizations tell us everything we need to know about the intensity and passion behind her interest: "anemone-like G-protein receptors embedded in cytoplasm, reaching out with their feathery arms. Ligands binding to the receptors by their curly tails, like sea dragons. Spiky tyrosine kinase receptors, awaiting the next signal." But Ellora goes further than that, explaining not just that she was enraptured by the shapes and colors, but the connection between the visuals and the process that she intellectually understands and is already intrigued by: how, she asks, can she use her newfound visualization of these processes in application to a different biological process, such as neural transmission? She visualizes that process of "folding proteins" as well, giving a comprehensive sense both of Ellora's artistic visualizations, her intellectual interests, and her ability to apply evidence to like situations, to draw analogies.

This synthesis of Ellora's visual experience and her application of it to her textbook intellectual interests is not only a clever observation about how visual aids and evidence enhance scientific understanding, but it also gives a very comprehensive sense of Ellora herself—not merely as a scientist, as someone interested in biological processes and labwork, but as someone who is wonderfully imaginative, strongly visual and, most brilliantly showcased here, a skillful writer, both in her descriptive and metaphorical ability and her ability to tie these purple passages to an analysis of a concrete moment of enlightenment and realization.

"Opening Up"

Shabnum Sukhi Gulati

Essay prompt: An intellectually engaging idea or experience

A FEW YEARS AGO, MY LIFE was perfectly compartmentalized. School was quantification and grades. "Me-time" was community service, the movies, and reading. "Real-life" was my job, concerns for the future, and my broken home. Debate was my escape. I viewed my arguments as regurgitated academia, strategically hyperbolic and used to prove a point. I saw them as informative and grounded in truth, but ultimately contrived and de-linked from my other planes of existence.

Before my fourth major national tournament, my coach sat down and handed me papers about racism. I stared at him. I was used to debating hypothetical nuclear war scenarios and internal mechanics of legislation. I was used to objectivity and personal distance from my advocacy. Debating the structural, systemic harm of racism was new territory. Debating the moral implications of legislation, especially racism, was personal. It reminded me of the discrimination I experienced before I moved to Maryland; it pushed me out of my comfortable world of utilitarian impact comparisons.

At first, I debated the arguments no differently than I would have debated the merits of U.S. hegemony. I was hesitant to use my personal experiences, to mix up worlds. As I continued to research the arguments, though, their reality slapped me. The racism that authors like Albert Memmi and Joseph Barndt talked about was not a myth. It was the same discrimination that I had lived through. In that instant I realized that it did not matter how much I wanted to keep all of the different parts of my intellectual being separate, I simply could not.

I stopped trying to compartmentalize. I allowed my personal passions to color how I articulated my arguments, and I started using what I learned from school and debate to improve my community service efforts. When I was forced to grasp the reality of my intellectual pursuits, I did much more than grow as an intellectual. I learned how to use that growth to progress in all aspects of my life.

ANALYSIS

The true success of this essay is that it balances simplicity and complexity, both in its message and in its technical structure, while illustrating the evolution of the writer's thoughts and feelings. From a narrative point of view, the plot is simple; the writer presents a situation (being a member of the debate team), a turn (confronting a difficult topic - racism) and a resolution (figuring out a new way to think about said topic). Of course, beneath the surface, Sukhi explains how her experience brought about a reexamination of her priorities, her debate strategies and ultimately, her own identity, before she is able to attain a new level of awareness.

Likewise, from a technical standpoint, the essay's building blocks are simple; the writer uses parallel syntax to create an easy-to-follow cadence of sentences. But taking a step back, these blocks, when stacked upon one another, build something greater, layer upon meticulous layer. This strong execution is what makes the essay so easy to digest and ultimately, what makes it so successful.

In the opening sentences, the writer introduces the different elements of her life in simple, basic terms: "School was…", "'Me-time' was…", "'Real-life' was…" and "Debate was…" Sukhi's straightforward language familiarizes the reader with the situation quickly and efficiently. The next two sentences offer reflection; the writer explains her emotional detachment from aspects of debate, but she keeps the rhythm tight by again employing parallel syntax by starting the sentences with "I viewed" and "I saw".

The next paragraph unfurls almost poetically. The writer observes, "my coach sat down and handed me papers about racism," and quickly follows with, "I stared at him." The short, staccato response captures the gravity of the moment, as if to portend the impossibility of the situation. The reader can almost feel the pause in the action as the writer stares at her coach. Moving on, the writer maintains symmetry in her syntax—"Debating the structural, systemic harm of racism was new territory. Debating the moral implications of legislation, especially racism, was personal." This led to two simple results: "reminding" the reader of discrimination and "pushing" her out of her comfort zone.

The essay reaches its climax in the third paragraph, as Sukhi opens the floodgates to her thoughts. Departing from the perfectly designed sentence structure of the first two paragraphs, the reader can almost feel the evolution of thought and perspective that the writer is chronicling. Gone is the parallel syntax, and instead, the writer piles thought upon new thought, ranging from an initial feeling of hesitancy, to a desire to research and learn more to the all important realization of a new understanding.

In the final paragraph, the writer unwinds the tension of her story and offers reflection. Returning to a kind of parallel sentence structure that is more fluid than that of the first two paragraphs, the reader can experience the growth the writer has undergone, both "as an intellectual" and "in all aspects of [her] life." The closing pace also allows the reader to take a moment to exhale.

When we read this essay once through, its message and its structure may strike us as interesting and at the very least, somewhat memorable. However, as we re-examine it, we can really begin to appreciate the artful skill with which it was composed. Perhaps our only critique is that the writer might have elaborated more on how exactly this lesson played out "in all aspects of [her] life". However, we realize that there is limited space in which to share these stories.

Overall, while this essay was written with a great deal of technical prowess, it is not fair to expect that your essay should match it element for element. In fact, no two successful essays are exactly alike, and this should be a reminder that what is most important is that you leverage your strengths a writer to make your true self shine in your essay. This writer happened to have a strong technical command of language and an interesting story to go along with it; your strength may be your humor, your energy or your poignancy. Whatever your strength is, find it, and like this writer, capitalize on it!

"A Letter to My Future Roommate"

Vienna Harvey

Essay prompt: A note to your future roommate

DEAR ROOMMATE,

Are you a cyborg? (Don't worry, I'll explain later.)

Obviously I can't say everything about me in a letter, so just a few basics. My name is Vienna (my parents met in Austria at Stanford Overseas). I always have trouble answering when asked where I'm from. I was born in Stockholm then lived in two different towns in Washington. When I was 8, my family moved aboard a sailboat and we spent 4 years circumnavigating (almost) North America. We eventually wound up in Norfolk, Virginia, where we've been ever since.

I've been homeschooled my whole life, but for the last few years I've been taking most of my classes at ODU as a non-matriculated student.

I haven't chosen a major yet. There's so much I'm interested in— from psychology, astronomy, law and archaeology to physics, acting, photography and writing, pretty much everything except math. There's always a new craft project I'm working on, a few books that I'm reading and a few more that I plan to read soon. I speak Spanish, take Irish dance, write hieroglyphs and recently took a trapeze class. In my CTY course this summer, we talked a lot about cyborgs and how to recognize them. Since then I've thought it might be cool to meet one.

Lots of people think I'm crazy. The homeschooling, the college classes, my eclectic interests and weird vocabulary… (I like collecting strange words. "Quisquilious" is my current favorite because it's so fun to say. It means "of, or pertaining to, trash or garbage.") Personally, I think everyone's a little crazy. Life would be boring without some craziness!

I hope you're not too much of a neat freak. My sister once said, "Vienna is like a vapor; sooner or later she'll fill up any space she's put into." That's a bit of an exaggeration but you get the idea. I can keep my room clean if I really try though.

So now I've told you a bit about me, what about you? Where are you from? What do you like to do? All that jazz…

See you soon!

Vienna

....

ANALYSIS

With so many essays beginning with "The most important thing to me…" any way you can change it up and write in a different format will set you apart (as well as give some relief to the reader). The "letter to a future roommate" format allows you to not only write in a more personal, colloquial tone but also to delve into the personality quirks, pet peeves and daily routines that make you a real human being.

Vienna takes advantage of the direct dialogue to present a portrait of herself that goes beyond a specific experience or academic record. Right away she throws you a curveball with "Are you a cyborg?"— which might pique interest or seem gratuitous, depending on how she pulls it off later in the letter. She also plugs her family's connection to Stanford while explaining her name, and universities *love* alumni.

Vienna gives enough information about herself to make you want to talk with her in person: living on a sailboat and circumnavigating North America? Sounds like an epic adventure, especially for child! Tell me more! Home schooled? How did that work on a boat? Or why continue home schooling back on land? Tell me more! Why don't you like math? How do you know how to write hieroglyphs? And how *do* you recognize a cyborg? Tell me more!

Vienna treads a fine line of sparking interest by mentioning a topic and teasing by not giving enough details as to *why* something is important. When talking about yourself, especially in a letter, it's easy to come across as boasting or self-centered, but Vienna does a good job of just presenting what she does / what she's like without sounding like a resume. A nifty trick is to have someone else read your letter out loud back to you so you can get a sense of how it sounds.

And while she says she's messy, the highly-organized essay and writing style reveals a similar mind. Notice the succinct yet multi-purpose penultimate paragraph: not only does she show (not tell) that she has a sister and can get along with others in a shared space ("I can keep my room clean if I really try though."), but she's chosen a "key quote" that describes her well beyond living-space tidiness.

What university wouldn't want someone like Vienna, with all her interests, abilities and experiences, to "fill up" their learning community space?

4

BOOKS/LITERATURE

"Pride and Prejudice"

Sumaya Quillian

Essay prompt: A note to your future roommate

YOU SHOULD KNOW NOW THAT JANE Austen is my favorite author. I love to talk about books, so you may expect her name to come up often, along with my favorite Austen novel *Pride and Prejudice*. I have read it so many times that I can recite parts of it by heart, and I do not love it just because it is witty and romantic and hilarious; I actually learned something from it. Whenever I think of that novel, I remember all the times I misjudged someone. I have deemed others to be arrogant, irritating, and impertinent within minutes of meeting them, and many times I have been completely mistaken. When I was in sixth grade, for instance, I thought one of the girls in my orchestra class seemed annoying, and she has become the best friend I have ever had.

First impressions are not reliable, and reading *Pride and Prejudice* made me realize how frequently I have depended on them. I have not always taken the time to understand and learn about a person before I formed an opinion, and that is a great injustice to any decent person. Eventually, I have always recognized when my judgments were wrong, but before I never thought about why they were wrong. Finally understanding the unfairness of my opinions has been one of the most important things I have learned about myself. It has made me more impartial and open-minded, and I have become better at learning from others. For both our sakes, I only improve at ignoring the tendency to form premature sentiments. We will be sharing a room for an entire school year, and I know how tiresome it would be if I were quick to judge.

ANALYSIS

Sumaya is dealing with a very limiting word count, and it does show in the vagueness of her otherwise-vivid and lavish details here—the example of the girl in her orchestra, for instance, might simply benefit from a name or the detail of an instrument. She is also treading very well-traveled territory, making Jane Austen's *Pride and Prejudice* the backbone of her essay. Sumaya does not necessarily add much in her interpretation of the novel, but the humor of her treatment of it and her adamant conviction about the importance of the novel's message to her own life make for a winning and memorable combination.

Sumaya, like others, starts out with a conversational tone, genuinely adhering to the essay's prescribed "letter" format. This allows Sumaya to address the reader casually and to let slip what seem like personal details, in the same way as she might to her actual roommate: the distinction she makes between liking a book because it is enjoyable and liking a book because it has taught her a lesson, for instance, provokes a smile, and her tone and paratactic style here lend themselves to her creation of a likeable and sympathetic persona: "I do not love it just because it is witty and romantic and hilarious; I actually learned something from it." Other confessions—the multiple times she has judged someone to be irritating or impertinent, her friend from orchestra—and her willingness to admit the number of times she has been wrong make Sumaya particularly likeable and reinforce the sense that this is a lesson she has, indeed, genuinely learned and genuinely works to correct.

Finally, Sumaya makes an excellent point in her second paragraph that demonstrates superior critical thinking skills, although she might have written it slightly more explicitly to really help her point hit home: "Eventually, I have always recognized when my judgments were wrong, but before I never thought about why they were wrong."

Sumaya goes from identifying single mistakes, such as the girl in orchestra whom she disliked, to, with the help of Jane Austen, understanding a pattern and identifying the underlying reactions and impulses that cause it. This point not only shows Sumaya's keen instinct but it also makes it clear that Jane Austen's Pride and Prejudice is not merely a contrived entrée to an essay, but in fact a really integral part of this revelation about Sumaya's tendency to form judgments and her efforts to thwart that tendency. She ends with a remark that brings us back to the format of the essay, and her return to direct address of the roommate is a clever move—it brings us back to the immediate context of the essay and, more importantly, the imminent situation of sharing a room, in which Sumaya promises to try not to be quick to judge. Her frankness and her direct reference to the situation at hand demonstrate Sumaya's ability on the one hand to think abstractly and in terms of patterns and themes, as well as her ability to apply that thinking to real-life situations, all of which would, the reader thinks, make Jane Austen proud.

"Truths Learnt from a Lie"

Anonymous

Essay prompt: An intellectually engaging idea or experience

"WRITING AND WAR: TIM O'BRIEN IN conversation with Tobias Wolff": this was a conversation I had to hear. I had loved *The Things They Carried*—the pages in my copy are covered in my scribbles, underlinings, and exclamation points—but I was dying to hear O'Brien's opinions in person. That night, the discussion centered on true stories—how you know they're true by that feeling in the pit of your stomach. I spent the entire presentation spellbound, wishing that I were a participant, that the comments and questions I wrote in my notebook would be discussed by the two authors on stage. As an occasional writer, I know how difficult it can be to convey my emotions to a reader solely through fact. Sitting in the audience that evening, however, I learned I didn't need to—the purpose of literature is not just to deliver accurate facts and stories but also to convey our irrational thoughts and illogical emotions—the true human experience. This knowledge has changed the way I view writing, both my own and others'.

Perhaps more important than what I heard and thought that evening, however, was simply the fact that I was there. About 500 people had decided to show up. Cubberly seats 400. But I had my heart set on hearing this discussion, and sitting out in the lobby wasn't what I'd planned. So when the doors were closing, and a woman guarding the entrance called, "High School groups only!", I took a breath, built up the courage, and approached her.

"Hi—excuse me, but my teacher is in there reserving a seat for me. Can I go in?"

I hesitate to consider my words a flat-out lie. At best, they could be classified as wishful thinking: my teacher had told me he would attend the presentation but I wasn't sure he had made it—he hadn't. There were no seats left, but I happily sat on the floor. A while later, the woman who had let me in walked by: I watched as recognition, frustration, understanding, and finally acceptance crossed her face. I smiled a guilty smile, and she moved on.

ANALYSIS

In "Truth Learnt from A Lie" the writer retells her experience seeing a conversation at a local university between two writers she admires. The tenacity and drive of the student is aware from the very first sentence of the essay; "Writing and War: Tim O'Brien in conversation with Tobias Wolff": this was a conversation I had to hear." With an infectious excitement, this student's essay sets a passionate tone.

The student conveys that attending this event was meaningful for her because of her love for the books produced by these writers and because of her personal interest in and practice with writing. The student was excited by the opportunity to see and hear two esteemed writers in person, and she relates her hopes of being stimulated by learning how O'Brien and Wolff thought about and created their work.

The unseen obstacle to attending the conversation between the two writers is the event was already at capacity when she arrived; the auditorium was closed to all except high school students. While this high school student admits to telling a half-truth in order to finagle her way into the auditorium, apparent from the situation are her perseverance, her enthusiasm for literature and her hunger for an intellectual experience. The student represents herself genuinely, but the student doesn't justify her actions, she honestly acknowledges that there was some deception, a gray area she took spontaneously took advantage of, but there's also a sense of the individual student's drive that comes through: she won't easily take no for an answer.

What makes this essay memorable is not only the extent to which the student wants to witness the authors' conversation, but her wish to be on the stage, to be sitting with the authors. Her wish illustrates the degree her ambitions, her activities and her dreams are aligned with intellectual fulfillment that also provides a personal fulfillment. It shows a student with a personal intellectual interest and highlights her enthusiasm to take advantage of the opportunities available in a college setting.

The student *does* make it inside the crowded auditorium. She deftly shares how the conversation between the two writers changed her outlook and views on writing; "the purpose of literature is not just to deliver accurate facts and stories but also to convey our irrational thoughts and illogical emotions—the true human experience." What she gleans from the conversation between the two writers could also be applied to her personal experience, which provides a nice resonance in the essay; the student writes about an experience here where her overwhelming desires and emotions led to a poignant experience for her.

Concisely, the student is able to demonstrate through the content of her writing her passions, her drive and her ability to learn and reflect. She also demonstrates a facility with language as the narrative reads clearly, earnestly and vivaciously. In writing an essay, this student wisely chose a prompt that recalled a special event in her life, one that she could convey well on the page. When writing an admissions essay, it's important to select a topic and subject that allows you to display your natural enthusiasm.

"Blur"

Anonymous

"ALL YOUR LIFE YOU LIVE SO close to truth, it becomes a permanent blur in the corner of your eye, and when something nudges it into outline it is like being ambushed by a grotesque." –Tom Stoppard in *Rosencrantz and Guildenstern are Dead.*

I leafed through the thin manuscript, soaking up the absurdity between its unconventional pages, drowning myself in hysterical fits of laughter. The next minute, a frown planted itself firmly on my face. A stubborn rascal of a thought had lodged itself into the reservoirs of my mind, prompted by Stoppard's rather "absurd" words.

Literature had always evoked questions in me, but this idea seemed different. I struggled with its implications—logic rendered it inherently incongruous, nature irrevocable. Could I no longer accuse the truth of evading me? Had it been the other way around all this time? "Guilty" carved itself across my forehead. My frantic shouts of protests seemed hollow, my attempts to understand the world feeble and half-hearted.

The stubborn rascal birthed stubborn-rascal-offspring who mistook my mind for their personal playground. As I rode home from school, my gaze, through the glare of the car window, reluctantly met stony eyes, empty expressions, faces outlined in grimaces: a chilling pantomime of wretchedness that painfully mocked my complacency. The realization that it entailed seemed inevitable, inescapable: "the permanent blur" in my vision dissolved into the stark clarity of calloused fingers on outstretched hands,"

"Think about all those Friday afternoons?" the stubborn rascal persisted, prodding his elbow into the sensitive underside of my belly. To me, a Friday afternoon meant a ride in my friend's pick-up truck, music blasting, shocks of laughter igniting the air. Through the corner of my eyes, I could see dark silhouettes of desperation lurking dangerously but I would ignore the disturbance in my vision, pretend it was a side-effect of my contact lens, and continue on as if nothing had happened. I wondered, could I once again blind my vision to the extent that the blur would simply cease to exist? Would I eventually look out the window and see nothing at all? Would the pang of emotions that struck me upon seeing the pantomime of human suffering, of inexplicable pain, melt into nothingness, indifference?

No. I refuse to be blinded. I will not hide from the "grotesque" truth that looms over me.

But I refuse to be jaded. I will not forget the other truths—the intimate truths I discover in my mother's quiet love, in my father's over-vigilant care, in the nonsensical language of shared jokes. The truths I discover in the joys of the sad city I have grown to love: the midnight snacks of *chat masalain,* the tumultuous streets, fries cooked by the roadside, in an evening at the beautiful beach. I will not forget these truths, truths that have been so good to me, truths that bind, that make me believe.

When a bomb destroyed an entire building this year, I was watching my school's production of *Romeo and Juliet*. When I reached home, I found out twenty people died between Act Two and Act Four. I was told they ended the night by singing "Heal the World."

I know that we need healing. I also know that there is something *worth* healing—because I believe.

ANALYSIS

The essay "Blur" begins with an epigraph from Tom Stoppard's *Rosencrantz and Guildenstern are Dead*. The essay uses this quote as a launching point for reflecting on the student's changed outlook, which is catalyzed by a reading experience. The student charts a change in her perception of self and the world she lives in. The quote makes her see she has lived in "complacency" with the human suffering around her, tuning out the misfortune of others. For the first time, the student is coming to an acute awareness that while she is enjoying life, others are experiencing great difficulties. This college essay attempts to acknowledge and chart the student's growing awareness of the incongruities of life experienced by herself and others

Immediately, the diction in "Blur" stands out as a unique aspect of the writing. The student's vocabulary is concise and aims for precision. Her facility with language is on display and reflects the sophistication of her thoughts. Overall, the language isn't out of register because the student seems comfortable with the vocabulary of her writing style. In writing a college admissions essay, one should feel comfortable to be oneself; use language in a way that feels natural to you. If your writing and speaking vocabulary includes words such as "feeble," "reservoirs," "incongruous" and "pantomime" as this student's does then allow yourself to express your thoughts and ideas using the vocabulary that is most familiar to you. No matter what kind of vocabulary you use, it's important to write in a voice that feels natural to you and not to pitch your writing too high or low because that's what you believe the admissions committee expects or would be impressed by.

The student's use of the epigraph from *Rosencrantz and Guildenstern are Dead* allows her to demonstrate her interest in literature and her ability to understand and engage the philosophical ideas of what she reads. The writer can show with this essay that her academic studies affect her consciousness and how she comprehends her life. In addition, the student takes advantage of the epigraph to intermingle her personal life with her academic life. She illustrates that she enjoys a social life, but also enjoys a *Romeo and Juliet* play; there's a personality here that's evident and it makes the widening vision of the speaker more relatable.

In the final paragraph of this essay, the writer reveals that while she's watching the play, *Romeo and Juliet,* a tragedy occurs in her city, a building is bombed. This event encapsulates the ruminations the speaker has been trying to deal with throughout the essay in a poignant and highly contrasting moment. While she's enjoying a Shakespeare play, other people are losing their lives. Ending on this note is somber but represents the student's desire to acknowledge the beauty and the devastations of reality. This striking story is somewhat undercut by the ambiguity of the situation as it's unclear why those who were killed in the bombing were singing "Heal the World." Perhaps the speaker could have provided more detail on the bombing to add context for the reader.

The final line of the essay is also overly general in its summary. There's a fear oftentimes that one needs to make sure one's essay writing has made a point, so abstract statements are used in summary, but it's important to avoid this pitfall. Summary statements should draw from the specific topics covered in the body of the essay.

5

CAREER

"A Patient Discovery"

Brian Tashjian

Essay prompt: An intellectually engaging idea or experience

PABLO'S EYES WERE WIDE WITH FEAR as he ran up to us on our way down the hill. Juan had fallen off the roof on the first day of repairs, while Mike and I were at breakfast half a mile up the hill in Diamonte. Juan was only semi-conscious and his wrist was swollen half way up his forearm. He was bleeding from his forehead and had a contusion on his right temple. A community member had carried him to his house and had laid him down in his bed, where he remained until we pushed through the crowd around him at his house. I worked my way next to his bed, asking the few people closest to him what had happened. "A bad beam of wood," they said, "Madera mala." Falling fifteen feet from the roof to the cement floor had fractured Juan's wrist and given him a concussion. Much to my dismay, he refused to go to the hospital for two weeks, with his wife supporting this decision. The rest of that day, the first day of the community project to repair the roof of the church,

I did everything I could to help the project's number one advocate and leader. I fed him water, cleaned and bandaged his wounds on his head and arm, and I was the only one communicating with him on where he hurt, the only one trying to convince everyone that he needed to go to the hospital. Right then, speaking Spanish was not a skill that I was learning or improving, the language came without hesitation, for grammar and structure became low priority. Sitting there at Juan's bedside, communicating with him as best I could and trying to do everything that I thought would help him, showed me how important it is to me to care for people for the rest of my life. This moment of realization sparked my interest in medicine, and it solidified my desire to help those in need either physically or mentally. But I want to be able to do more than I did then; I want to gain the experience to be able treat my patients as well as I can before having to send them to the hospital.

ANALYSIS

Brian's essay builds interest from the very start. His first line is a great example of a "hook" that sparks curiosity. Brian manages to maintain a high level of intensity throughout his narration, since the situation he writes about has a lot of inherent drama. The techniques he uses apply to all storytelling, though, not just spinning a high-stakes yarn like this one. He conjures up an easy-to-visualize scene of a crowd gathered around Juan's bed and conveys a sense of urgency as he describes how he "pushed through the crowd" to see Juan. He also provides specific details, most notably in the long sentence, "I fed him water, cleaned and bandaged his wounds on his head and arm, and I was the only one communicating with him on where he hurt, the only one trying to convince everyone that he needed to go to the hospital." Effective vignettes like this one use vivid verbs, provide relevant detail and communicate what is at stake in the story. In this case, it is obvious that the stakes are high. Nonetheless, even in a more mundane story, such as a tale about a challenge you faced at school, you have to show that what goes on in the story has significant consequences—even if they are internal and/or personal. If the reader cannot sense what's at stake in the story, he or she has no reason to care about what happens.

Besides telling a compelling story, Brian lets the reader know some compelling facts about himself. He shows that he took a remarkable amount of initiative in caring for Juan. He also lets readers see that he has gained an important skill, the ability to speak Spanish, but that he values that skill not only on an academic level or for bragging rights, but rather for the concrete impact it allows him to have on those around him. Finally, he gets across the idea that he has good reasons for wanting to study medicine. Almost anyone pursuing that path will write that they want to study medicine in order to help people, but few can work in a relevant example to show that they have direct experience with a patient and clear motivation for wanting to help in a concrete way. Brian's essay succeeds both at the level of storytelling and at the level of personal revelation.

6

CHALLENGES

"No, *This* is Who I Am"

Annelis Breed

I AM A CHILD OF DIVORCED parents. My biological father is not available to me emotionally or financially. My mother remarried when I was still young. Our five-and then six-person blended family lived on my stepfather's family farm, in a two bedroom singlewide trailer, which was a tight fit. Looking back, I know my family was dysfunctional, but it seemed "normal" to me. Life was fairly decent in my elementary and middle school years. But there has been little peace or ease throughout my high school years.

My freshman year was especially difficult for me. My grandmother legally revoked her permission for my family to live on the farm after my grandfather passed. After thirteen years, the move was abrupt. We ended up homeless, living in a single hotel room.

My sophomore year, my mom home schooled me, expecting to transfer me into a public high school. What started as temporary, grew into a whole school year; we were homeless for six months. There were no A.P. or Honors classes, but I tried taking as many courses as I could, in an effort to stay competitive academically.

My junior year started at Mount Vernon High School. Finding a house was a relief, but my parents became obsessed with keeping me away from other teenagers. I was not allowed to stay after school for anything. They liked to feel in control of me. By the end of the school year, they were punishing me by making me sleep on the living room floor and sending me outside; my mom would set food on the porch. I was allowed back into the house again until 8:00 at night, when I was allowed a shower. Except for sleeping, I lived outside, eating and doing my homework. I began to feel like an animal, kept outside and rejected as if unwanted. School was a relief. It was a tricky balancing act to keep good grades, and I barely hung on emotionally.

With my school counselor, I finally decided to file a CHINS petition (Child in Need of Services). The petition, if passed, would remove me from my parents' home. The judge who looked at the paperwork removed me from my home immediately. I left that day for Bellingham, where my god family lives, with only the dirty clothes on my back. Eventually, after hearing the case, the county commissioner suggested emancipation instead, since I was almost eighteen.

As my senior year begins, I look forward to new opportunities. I'll be a new student for the fourth time in my high school career, but I'm determined to succeed and thrive. I am taking four AP classes, run on the cross-country team, and am in a couple clubs. My personal struggles are not reflected on my transcript; I am proud of that. My experiences have prepared me for college, adulthood, and life. My past neither restricts nor obstructs me; it simply has helped shaped me into the person I am.

ANALYSIS

The first sentence of this essay hits you hard. Short and to the point, abrupt and unexplained, Annelis' first sentence shocks the reader although the fact that her parents are divorced itself is not that uncommon. Still, this sentence properly sets the tone for the rest of essay, which becomes more intense as it continues, unraveling more and more detail about the Annelis' life during high school.

Talking about hardships as grave as Annelis' in a college admissions essay is a difficult task to accomplish. A dark essay runs the risk of alienating the reader, or making him/her feel uncomfortable. However, especially in this case, an essay about difficult life circumstances can also give admissions officers a lot of detailed information about conditions that may have affected grades or minimized participation in extracurricular activities.

Annelis walks the fine line of giving all the details necessary without going overboard. She does this by being precise and to the point. She gives all the facts in an appropriate amount of detail, explaining how and why she was forced to live outside during her junior year. However, Annelis is careful to not spend too much time talking about her feelings. In this way, she prevents her essay from being a rant, full of self-pity. Instead of blaming anyone, Annelis simply explained what happened, step-by-step, from beginning to end.

The concise nature of Annelis' writing makes it easier to process. She hints at being in a state of turmoil when she notes that she "barely hung on emotionally," but she sticks to discussing facts that are sincere, honest and measurable. Ultimately, Annelis' essay hits the perfect balance between being informative and evocative. The reader sympathizes with Annelis, but not enough that it is difficult to think about the facts of her situation, or what it means for her as a collegiate candidate. It is clear as to why she was not able to take many AP or honors classes early in high school, but those facts do not inform us how Annelis will handle herself academically in college.

In her final paragraph, Annelis begins to discuss in more detail what her situation means for her future. She lightens the tone of the essay by discussing her drive and her willingness to engage in the new opportunities available to her. Un-intimidated by her past, she takes on a rigorous academic load of 4 AP classes on top of several extracurricular activities. Her positive attitude and ambition despite hardship prove that she is able to over come incredible adversity. Even before she explicitly says it, Annelis shows us why she is truly able to deal with any of the obstacles she may face in college. Furthermore, her confidence instills a sense of hope in the reader. By the end, all we want is for Annelis to succeed.

"A Picture Is Worth a Thousand Words: My Piano"

Ellora Karmarkar

I LOVE SITTING NEXT TO MY cousin as he strums the sarod. The flowing sounds of music wash over me and make me feel whole. Sometimes, my mind pulls apart his songs, trying to figure out the musical patterns so that I can learn and recreate them. Usually, though, I just listen, knowing that I can feel my cousin's emotion and devotion through the quality of his tone. His love for the sarod represents the most precious part of music to me. I have realized my piano is important to me in a similar way. Its shiny keys are the first friends I tell my secrets to, the best mode for expressing my thoughts and feelings. It's hard for me to believe that I almost lost this crucial part of my life when I was twelve.

It was supposed to be just a regular day, as I chowed down on my breakfast before I headed off to school. Yet, I just had to see that letter lying on the table. It was from my new piano teacher, ___. She was supposed to turn me into a concert pianist, something I fervently desired, as well as help me for my piano competition season.

I was hopeful, though I found her methods odd. My fingers were itching to stroke the keys, but most of her lessons were spent correcting my posture. She killed my free spirit. I became a cardboard cutout, very shy and obedient. Her instructions were law. Then came the letter, addressed to my mother. It beckoned me. "Never read mail addressed to your mother," the good girl inside me whispered. It was already open. Surely nobody would notice if I just peeked. I opened it.

"She has a very simple mind. I have to keep teaching her the same thing every week." My eyes widened. "I'm sure I can continue teaching her, but she has no real future in music. She has no talent—"

I believed every word. 'I have no talent.' I started to cry. I didn't speak to anyone that day because I was too ashamed. I felt I wasn't good enough for my piano anymore. I thought that everyone else had lied to me when they told me I had great potential. That evening, I tried to play one of my favorite pieces to see if there was any glimmer of hope for me. My fingers kept stumbling along the keys. It sounded clumsy and contrived. The perfectionist in me was disheartened. Frustrated, I slammed my fist into my best friend, and its piano keys jangled with distress. I stormed away. I didn't touch the piano for days and was close to giving up music entirely.

My teacher quit the same week because she felt I was a waste of time. My mom started to panic. With her friend's timely recommendation, I was set up with ___. With ___'s encouragement, I gradually realized that (first teacher)'s words were irrelevant. The crucial thing was that I loved music. Music had been such an important part of my life that I decided I wasn't ready to sacrifice it yet. He taught me to let my feelings race through my fingers instead of bottling them up in my mind. Each piece I played gained more color and depth once I poured myself into it. I started opening up again, slowly. My enthusiasm returned, though I was still doubtful about my future in music. I worked hard, trying to forget what (first teacher) had said.

I took a risk and continued working towards the piano competition. Competitions had been my great love when I was younger. After that painful experience, however, I was nervous about competing because I thought I might prove (first teacher) right. When we drove to my first competition of the season, my hands became clammy and tight. I calmed down once I entered the building. My motives were only to see what I was capable of. I let my emotions shine through the music when I was called up to play. While the judges deliberated, I recognized that I had enjoyed myself so much onstage that I didn't care about the outcome. I sighed with relief as the judges reentered. It didn't matter if somebody else won. To my great surprise, the judges awarded me first prize. My doubts about my future with music gradually subsided. The gift that music has given me will always be here.

I love being able to express my feelings in this beautifully complex form, like my cousin does. I adore drowning in dream-like nocturnes and brilliant sonatas alike. Though my sense of perfectionism gets in the way of my enjoyment sometimes, I'm glad that I kept struggling to learn. All of the hopeful energy I invested into music helped me become a better, stronger person. I no longer let myself back down in the face of other people's opinions. Whenever I see my piano, I'm reminded to keep up the fight for what I love, and to celebrate the life it gives me.

ANALYSIS

The longer essay presents a perfect opportunity to tell a story of a change or a transformative event, as Ellora does here. With more complex story lines comes more opportunity to explore more artistic themes as well, but also presents the greater challenge of juggling multiple events, times, insights and thematic devices. Ellora tells a smart story here, one almost so subtle that it escapes the reader the first time around—she explains how she came to not simply redis-cover her love for piano, but to become more comfortable with her love of the emotion of music rather than the technical prowess she was previously striving for. She isn't overt with that "thesis," if you will, but rather slips it in: she mentions her "fervent desire" to become a concert pianist that fuels her as she studies with her first teacher, and then describes how her second teacher helps her to let her feeling guide her music-making and ultimately helps Ellora to access what it is in music that she truly loves. But Ellora tells her story in an even smarter way: with essays that are longer and more complex, covering a greater expanse of narrative time, it can often be helpful to do what Ellora does here and present a sort of "preview" of the end result at the beginning. Ellora does it artfully by analogy to her cousin's musical skills and her admiration of them. She begins with a lovely and obviously carefully composed description of his music and an analysis of why Ellora enjoys his playing—her rather loose and impressionistic description reinforces the sense that it is not so much his technical skill as his emotion that she admires.

Ellora then alerts her readers that we are going to move back in time: the reflections on her cousin's music are her current perspective, but when she says, "It's hard to believe I almost lost this crucial part of my life when I was twelve," she transitions the readers to look back on Ellora's twelve-year-old self. We then see Ellora struggling to achieve the kind of technical prowess her first teacher demands of her in order to become a concert pianist—the rigidity of her teacher's instruction, the curtness of Ellora's description of it contrasts sharply with Ellora's introduction.

The story that Ellora then tells, of her despair at her first teacher's rejection and her eventual pairing with her second teacher, the comfort she feels as he lets her use her emotions to guide her music, has already been previewed in the introduction of the essay. The audience feels increasingly comfortable with Ellora's piano teacher and her relationship with music as it begins to conform more to the views she set out at the beginning of the essay, just as twelve-year-old Ellora felt more comfortable with her teacher and ultimately with her relationship to and goals within the field of music.

Ellora combines this clever structural strategy with lush descriptions and vivid details, stylistic tweaks that reinforce the emotions that she herself is feeling in the narrative—making for a memorable, genuine and well-composed essay.

"My Turning 'Pointe'"

Anonymous

MY MOM DIDN'T THINK IT WOULD last. I was not a child who cared about clothes, or brushing my hair for that matter. Pulling on pale pink tights with the finesse of an impatient seven-year-old and enduring the pain required to get my unruly hair slicked back into a bun was bound to be a recipe for failure. Yet for some reason that tedious daily routine soon evolved into a passion for classical ballet. I loved the structure and discipline that Miss W., our 67-year-old English ballet director, demanded. As a piano student, I loved listening to the talented accompanist play in the corner of our dusty, sea- foam green studio. I loved putting on beautiful costumes and gazing up at the advanced dancers who, only in high school, seemed decades older. My dream of going professional blossomed with age, and ten years later, I was the one who was admired.

A Chopin waltz lingers in the studio air as Miss W. suddenly stops the accompanist. We are in the midst of rehearsing Les *Sylphides* and someone must have stepped too far out of their line.

"No, no, no, girls", Miss W. scolds as she yanks yet another dancer back into her proper place. She storms out of the room, offended that her dancers had put *Les Sylphides* to shame with a sprinkling of mistakes. As Miss W. exits, we hear her call out, "Emily*, we must speak after rehearsal." I wasn't struggling with this part of the ballet and now the other dancers were eyeing me with curiosity. What could I have done? After two very long hours, I apprehensively step into Miss W.'s office.

I'm too short; my legs and arms are not long enough; my arches are not as high as they should be. Although Miss W. reveals these "truths" to me gently, I am shocked. After years of hard work and dedication to the art, ballet was my dream. To be told that the world of professional ballet does not want someone like me is the hardest thing I have ever been asked to accept.

At first, I fought this idea. I was just going to work harder, attain better technique, sharper turns, and higher leaps. But as I worked even harder in the studio, I began to realize the true source of my passion. I did not love ballet for the costumes, for the performing, or for the spotlight. My satisfaction came from the challenge and from those moments of accomplishment while dancing for myself. When I flawlessly executed a triple pirouette en pointe, I knew something inside of me had changed. My overwhelming desire to dance as the prima ballerina of a famous company had vanished, and my unquestionable love for both the art and the music took its place. I am proud of what I have learned, of what I have accomplished, and of what I have become. I no longer need the affirmation of a director to tell me otherwise.

* Name changed.

ANALYSIS

Even before she begins her essay, the writer of "My Turning 'Pointe'" pulls us into her world of ballet: she takes the essay prompt of describing a significant event or turning point in her life and makes it immediately relevant to her story with a balletic reference. And *story* is an apt description of her essay: the writer is able to both entertain and inform through a well-written and focused personal narrative that paints a distinct portrait of herself without sounding like a list of accomplishments or a resume.

The first paragraph not only paints a picture of the young ballerina but also demonstrates her ability to write engaging, well-structured prose. Her first line, "My mom didn't think it would last," intentionally uses a vague pronoun to engage the reader by wondering what "it" could be. Artful use of diction and alliteration—"Pulling on pale pink tights" and "slicked back into a bun was bound to be a recipe for failure"—as well as tripartite repetition—"I loved the structure..." "I loved listening..." "I loved putting on beautiful costumes..."—conveys her awareness and ability of the writing craft better than any list of English classes taken or literary classics read. Within a few lines, the writer creates the complex world of ballet and her place within it.

Notice how the writer drives each paragraph with a play of narrative rather than a "topic sentence": not a bad strategy to ensure interest, as application readers look over *hundreds* of essays at a time. We, the readers, are able to "walk a mile" in her shoes. The danger, however, lies in letting the story or scene overshadow the main subject: the middle three paragraphs of the essay focus on the situation with very little learned about the writer herself. However, the writer brings it back to both herself and the focus of the essay: the most difficult moment in her life, which transitions well into her reflection.

The writer returns to her title in the concluding paragraph, stating, "When I flawlessly executed a triple pirouette en pointe, I knew something inside of me had changed." Not only is she showing the fruits of her labor (even though there's no point in continuing professionally), but she's also sharing with us her reflection of the experience and how it's contributed to her as a person today. While it would have been great to know what the writer wants to pursue in the future, her dedication to dance and the self-confidence learned signals success to whatever she turns her mind (and body). If her other essays are as well-written and engaging as this one, taken together they present a multi-faceted and complex portrait of the artist as a young woman.

7

COMMUNITY SERVICE

"How I Got Started in Humanitarianism"

Anonymous

Essay prompt: What matters to you, and why?

THE SUMMER BEFORE MY FRESHMAN YEAR, I was lucky enough to visit Cambodia. While in Phnom Penh, I spent a day poorly building school benches, tolerably painting classrooms, and decently teaching English to a class of energetic 8 year-olds. They seemed like any other kids I had met: rambunctious, devious, and fun. I learned, however, that most of these students went home to houses without clean drinking water and that diseases from bacteria in the water were very common. These children live in the capital city! Living in the United States, we often lose perspective of our good fortune and how easy our life is: we have the luxury of clean running tap water in our homes—something that many residents of Cambodia's largest city and economic center do not have. Later I found out that $200 was enough to build a well that would provide 4-5 families with clean water. I took this idea to Stand Up! Speak Up! (SUSU), a club at my school devoted to raising awareness about human rights violations worldwide and to donating funds to try to combat the damage. That year we held a presentation on the Khmer Rouge and the Cambodian genocide, a terrible ordeal that surprisingly few students knew about, and this year we raised enough money to build two wells in Cambodia.

I have been an active member of SUSU for four years and am now the president. Throughout these years, we have invited speakers, held presentations, shown documentaries, and donated to multiple causes, all while increasing awareness in our school. For me, however, SUSU is more than just a way to advocate and promote human rights: it is a way for me to live more than just a self-absorbed life. Through the actions of the club, I make a difference, albeit a small one, in the lives of underprivileged people. I know that there are billions of impoverished and suppressed people in the world, but I believe that doing nothing, continuing on in our bubble of privilege without even attempting to help, is an injustice in itself.

ANALYSIS

This essay is an outstanding example of how to write about service because it relates how the author translated outrage into action. It may seem like the "wow" factor here is the trip to Cambodia in and of itself. Of course, traveling clear across the globe to serve others can be evidence of commitment, and of real gumption to boot. But the travel alone isn't eye-catching to admissions officers, especially given the rising popularity of international service trips. Instead, what stands out is the author's ability to act on her eye-opening experience in Cambodia through awareness-raising activities in the United States. Infinitely more impressive than the fact that she went Cambodia is what she did when she returned.

The author keeps a healthy sense of perspective about what she has done to help, demonstrating that her optimism about helping others is not mere pie-in-the-sky idealism. She keeps a sense of humor about her contributions while in Cambodia, where she spent time "poorly building school benches, tolerably painting classrooms, and decently teaching English." This line is particularly important, since it shows that she doesn't inflate the significance of going abroad to serve a foreign community. She understands that her impact was limited by her short time there and by the limited skills she brought to her tasks. Keep this approach in mind if you are ever tempted to puff up your own efforts while on a service trip. In the essay's final two lines, the author again acknowledges her limitations—"I make a difference, albeit a small one"—while affirming the importance of doing what you can to help.

She maintains a matter-of-fact tone in describing how she rallied her classmates back in the States to help improve conditions in Cambodia. After all, the initiatives she led are fairly simple: an assembly and a fund-raising drive. Nonetheless, they had an important impact both on her school and on clean water supplies in Cambodia. She uses these two efforts to segue into a more general discussion of her long-term role in Stand Up! Speak Up! and her position as president. Since she has already introduced the concrete example of her drive to improve access to clean water in Cambodia, her work in SUSU becomes more than just one more activity listed on an application. The author shows that she is perceptive enough to identify injustices, analytical enough to research good solutions, personable enough to gather support and educate her peers and practical enough to organize concrete interventions, like fundraising for well-building.

It may seem as if simply listing your service experiences will be enough to win the admiration of readers, but you must also demonstrate why you serve and what service means to you. The author here not only details her activism on one particular cause but also articulates a wider philosophy of service. For her, service is a "way...to live more than just a self-absorbed life" and to stand up to injustices, rather than standing idly by. If you're looking for a way to highlight your own service work, try following her lead by providing both an example of what you've done and the philosophy that inspired you to do it.

"Dominican Republic"

Devin K.

JUNE 20. I STEPPED OFF THE plane and walked down the long corridor, desperately trying to hold back tears. The beating in my head intensified as the sound of my friends' laughter slowly drowned out. I felt alone. I saw the familiar sight of home, but in the midst of wealth and comfort, came an overwhelming emptiness. My face grew hot and my tears tasted bitter on my dry tongue. The joy of my parents contradicted my extreme sadness, and at the sight of their smiling faces, the floodgates of my emotions burst open. My parent's expressions turned from excitement to confusion as I ran into my father's arms sobbing. I managed to say to them, "I have to go back! I have to take you with me! You don't understand; you don't know. I can't forget them...we have to help them."

My peers felt sheer elation upon returning home from the Dominican Republic; I, however, felt utter devastation. Home to the amenities and affluent environment of North San Diego, I felt guilty that I live in privilege while they suffer. My only desire was to get right back on a plane and take my parents with me back to the island to share with them the travesty I had just witnessed.

I have been on two mission trips to the Dominican Republic that radically changed my life. People often say that the greatest fulfillment one can receive comes through serving others, and I have experienced this personally through serving the people of the Dominican Republic. I was absolutely shocked by the overwhelming needs of the Dominican people. The hardships they endure are unbelievable especially to us Americans who live in the land of plenty. We see this suffering on the television, on commercials and in movies but to witness it first hand is something completely different. Young children are having children of their own, and with no husband, no job and no way to care for their babies, these abandoned teenage mothers are forced to rummage for food in the local landfills, and sometimes even resort to prostitution as a source of income. The young mothers are so unhealthy themselves that they are unable to produce milk for their newborns, thus infant mortality is incredibly high. These children are diseased, malnourished, uneducated, and hopeless, and many will eventually fall prey to the growing condition of human trafficking on the island. The children, however, see the good in every situation and I find it ironic that we Americans who have so much can be so unsatisfied, yet the Dominican people find happiness in the simplest toy or smile or hug. They live in extreme poverty, disease, destitution, and danger, yet somehow possess abounding joy and love.

My team and I abandoned the comforts of home to serve the Dominican people in the dangerous slums of Juan Dolio and give back a bit of the abundant blessings that we enjoy living in America. We conducted day camps in local orphanages and impoverished sugar-cane villages. The children played and sang songs with us and we brought donations for the families, and fed the young ones a hearty meal everyday. It was heartbreaking to see their distended bellies from malnourishment and worse to see some of the children refuse to eat their lunches, denying their own hunger to take the sandwiches home to feed their younger siblings or mommies. Seeing the gratitude on their precious, little faces was priceless, and the love that they showed us was unique and powerful. They were filled with emotion when we presented each of them a Polaroid picture of themselves, as many of the children had never seen their own image in a photograph, and some of the elders in the community even stood in line for their opportunity to pose for the camera. Serving the Dominican people is truly the greatest gift I have ever received and they have changed my outlook on life forever.

I have learned to be thankful for everything in my life because, the things I take for granted like running water, paved roads, sewer systems, my school, and clothing are luxuries to the Dominican people. While my biggest concern is college applications and extracurricular activities, those young children have to worry about basic needs such as where they are going to get their next sip of water, where they will sleep tonight and if they will wake up tomorrow morning. They have to cope with the cruel realities of living in a third world country where they have to fight daily for survival. I am grateful that I was given the opportunity to go on these mission trips because I now have a better understanding of the suffering, poverty, and injustice that occurs in this world. Upon returning from my first mission trip to the Dominican Republic, my greatest fear was that I would forget what I had witnessed. That I would fall back into my comfortable life and become desensitized once more to the suffering just beyond our borders. But, now I know that there is no way I can forget those people and, though I do not plan to be a missionary in the Dominican Republic, I seek to in some way bring help and hope to the Dominican people.

ANALYSIS

Based on topic alone this essay is truly powerful. The author shares an emotional experience in an artfully written and insightful way. She does an amazing job on a topic that if not done right, can come across as disingenuous. It's important to be very careful when writing about service trips in college essays for a handful of reasons. First, there are a lot of them: many people send in these types of essays and it takes a special one to stand out. Second, if not written in way that is both delicate and sophisticated they can backfire, inadvertently portraying the author as sheltered or immature. Finally, when not developed with the same level of insight and genuine sense of reflection as this one is, this type of essay comes across as forced or fake.

One of the things Devin did to make this essay special and genuine was simply tell the story. She opens the essay describing her emotional release when she arrived back to the U.S., a place that foiled the poverty and destitution of where she had just been. From there she talks about the people of the Dominican Republic, reflecting a true connection with the people and an understanding of their situation. Importantly, though she mentioned what service she did, purposely making the essay about the people of the Dominican Republic. This served to show that she was genuinely touched by the people she met, and she wasn't trying to paint herself as a hero for helping them—instead she just told their story. She also does an excellent job of describing how the trip touched her without overdoing it. This is the point at which many students fumble these types of essays because one runs the risk of sounding like: "I learned from the disadvantaged people that you don't need Gucci and Prada to be happy." While this quote is somewhat exaggerated, it reflects the most common pitfall on the service trip essay. What can be learned from this author's example is that expressing the way you were touched emotionally can really be the best way to remain genuine.

Overall this essay is a very strong written work. Exhibiting a strong command of varied vocabulary and syntax, the author developed an essay that should be used as a model for anyone who seeks to write the service essay without making some of the most common errors.

"Most Meaningful Extracurricular Activity"

Ellora Karmarkar

I WAS WORRIED WHEN WE SERVED the psychiatric patients food for Thanksgiving last year. It was my first time there and I wasn't quite sure how to act. I was scared that one of the patients might hurt me unintentionally. I scanned the room. My eyes lit up when they fell on the little black piano hiding in the corner.

While my mom served the meal to her patients, I slid onto the bench quietly and began to play. The room quieted down. I was so absorbed that I didn't notice the people gravitating towards the piano. However, in one of the pauses in the piece, I looked up and noticed that I was surrounded. I suddenly realized I was unsupervised. The pause went on longer than it was supposed to. I smiled nervously. A tall man next to the piano wearing a tattered green suit and an elf hat smiled back. "Keep playing. It sounds so nice." I calmed down and kept playing. A grin broke out on my face as several people started tapping their feet.

I have always loved to teach and share knowledge, but this exchange of enthusiasm for music was rare and powerful. I had never played for an audience like this. They made me feel like I was sharing something precious. I realized how foolish my fear was. We were all people, connected by the power of music. It touched me when they thanked me after I finished. I felt I should thank them. These patients showed me what sharing enthusiasm really meant.

ANALYSIS

This essay packs quite a lot into a very brief space: not only does it give us the barebones factual information about Ellora's extracurricular activities, serving meals in a psychiatric ward with her mother, but it also gives us a sense of Ellora's other interests, showcases her writing skills and makes a memorable point about a learning experience that is genuine, honest and smart.

Certainly the piece is centered on Ellora's community service, and the details that Ellora gives about it—it's Thanksgiving, and she is here with her mother—allow us to see that this seems to be more to Ellora than a line on her CV. Instead she fleshes out an otherwise nondescript resume item with thoughtful and specific details: it's a family affair, and it's meaningful enough to her and her family for them to be there on Thanksgiving.

But the particularly gracious aspect of Ellora's essay is that she understands the activity as meaningful not simply because she is doing it, but because of what it teaches her, both about other people, markedly different from herself, and herself. The community service setting simply serves to be the background for a more meaningful and more thought-provoking experience for her. This is a smart tactic from any point of view: centering the response around a single event or activity allows for clearer, more focused and efficient writing and the so-crucial specific details that make an applicant into a human being. Ellora does not simply focus on what it is she has to offer to the psychiatric patients in playing for them: she focuses on what they have to teach her, and it is this unique and generous—and consequently memorable—sentiment that is particularly catching when she says, "They made me feel like I was sharing something precious.... It touched me when they thanked me after I finished. I felt I should thank them." Ellora's memory of details is not only helpful for the reader to envision the scene, but it is also uniquely generous: she doesn't recall the piece she played, the composer, but she remembers what the patients are wearing, that the man was tall—which is a particularly striking and thus effective deployment of specific details in a short essay that allows very little room for superfluous descriptors.

Ellora also goes out on a limb in what she has to say: she confides that she was frightened, nervous, about the psychiatric patients. It could be potentially very off-putting to disclose that Ellora is uncomfortable around people so different from herself, but Ellora's generosity and honesty throughout her essay make her likeable, and the ultimate conclusion of her essay belies her initial skittishness. Stylistically, Ellora enhances the sense of her nervousness and complements her frankness with a succinct, paratactic style. She uses short sentences, bereft of detail, almost a little repetitive, with little subordination to each other: "I was worried when we served the psychiatric food for Thanksgiving last year... I was scared that one of the patients might hurt me unintentionally. I scanned the room." These continue as her nervousness resurfaces: "I looked up and noticed that I was surrounded. I suddenly realized I was unsupervised. The pause went on longer than it was supposed to. I smiled nervously." As Ellora feels more at home, her sentences get longer and more syntactically complex; her thoughts are more connected—almost like a shift in a piece of music. Her staccato sentences return at the end: "I felt I should thank them." But now they are short sentences coming from a place of confidence and security, leaving the reader feeling like they have completed a journey along with her.

"To Be Human"

Marisa G. Messina

Essay prompt: What matters to you, and why?

THE YEARNING LOOK IN HER EYES when she gazed at me through the unfinished window mattered to me. I could see years of despair dulling her vision, but now also a hint of hope glimmering somewhere, hardly visible beneath her mud-caked hair. That look made all the sweat on my face disappear. My sore arms ceased aching. My heart grew.

I was in Thailand with a group of twenty high school students. It was raining, and the heavy drops beat through the humid air and plopped on the tin roof of her shack next door.

My team and I were ensuring that it was one of the last rainy days this woman would spend living in a falling-apart shack. We built her house from the ground up: packed down the dirt foundation, mixed the concrete, laid the cinderblock walls. My body throbbed as I hauled 2x4s; my heart raced with both exhaustion and exhilaration at being able to provide her—and nine other families—with homes they had only dreamed of having. It mattered to me that my hands were giving back.

I'm fortunate: I landed in a family that loves me and that provides richness in my opportunity-laden life. But I know that few are this lucky. As a citizen of the world, it is my responsibility and my pleasure to contribute some compassion and aid to the common mosaic of human experience.

There is no better way for me to fathom the triumphs and troubles of my fellow humans than to inhabit their vantage points. These experiences channel my empathy and expand my understanding of what it means to be human and why it matters.

ANALYSIS

From the essay's very first word, Marisa transports us into the thick of the scene. Skipping introductions, she cuts right to the woman's "yearning look" and tells us that it mattered. "Why?" we wonder. Using simple yet brilliantly vivid language, she goes on to see "years of despair dulling her vision" and hope "hardly visible beneath her mud-caked hair." She sets the tone of meager means surrounding her, but we don't know who's who or what's going on. Her "arms ceased aching" and her "heart grew," and we feel some tension release by the end of the first paragraph. We get the sense the writer is there to do good, but we still don't know why.

Marisa continues to build momentum for a little longer, calling out the rain's "heavy drops [beating] through the humid air." Collectively we sit in suspense, waiting for some explanation. Finally, eight sentences in, the writer shares her mission: she and her peers are here to build this woman a new hew house. Aha! The big reveal offers answers to the questions we had throughout the opening, and now we have context for the scene being painted. Like the house the writer is literally building, we can mentally piece together the descriptions of what's happened and build a proper set of expectations—a blueprint, if you will—for what is still to come.

The writer does not disappoint in her delivery. With percussive, grounded descriptions of diligent movement and toil, she brings the reader along as her body "throbs" through the strenuous tasks of construction. We now understand why she would put her body through such stress, and also why the payoff seems to take away any physical pain whatsoever.

And just as we think our protagonist may lose her footing and turn this essay into a brag sheet of her accomplishments, she lays bare her humility, reminding us that she grew up "fortunate" but that she can appreciate how blessed she truly is. It is at this point that Marisa makes the boldest statement of the essay. Identifying herself as a "citizen of this world," she articulates her idea of her worldly duty—"to contribute some compassion and aid to the common mosaic of human experience." We will say that she took a slight risk in proclaiming this as the duty of all global citizens, essentially guilt-tripping those of us who *aren't* contributing such compassion and aid, but we like the conviction with which she says it.

The writer closes by tying all the pieces together—the woman whose house she and her peers are building, the disparity between their means and the simultaneous pain and joy of giving back—by assigning a greater meaning to it all. She proclaims that to understand and to give back is to be human, and that this experience matters not only to her, but to humanity itself.

The reason this essay is so effective is that it oozes with passion and energy, and the writer shares her experience in such simple, straightforward terms that we relate not just to the cause, but to the very blood, sweat and tears shed at the scene. The writer doesn't need to give the entire backstory (Who is this woman? How did she get to Thailand? What happens in the aftermath?), because she has already made us care about the plain black-and-white dynamics in play. This woman is poor. The writer is an able-bodied young woman. She is here with her peers to bring her some sort of basic, human provisions and security. There is no logical argument the reader can make that would question the writer's actions because we experience the woman and her poverty as real.

Building this rock solid foundation, like the house the protagonists are building, offers us a framework in which to appreciate his work. The reflections she makes even spur us to examine our own priorities—What can I do to give back? Within these few hundred words, we feel we have quite a strong understanding of what makes this young woman tick, and it only makes us feel good about her.

8

FAMILY

"Standing on the Shoulders of Giants"

Olutosin Sonuyi

I BELIEVE THAT IN ORDER TO be a respected and productive member of society one must have a steadfast set of values. In a world where an incalculable number of influences, distractions, and pressures exist, it is crucial that we have stabilizing, enduring forces in our lives. In my life I have been able to lean on my family to guide me towards the right path.

In a way, one might consider my life comparable to the mechanism of a gyroscope. A gyroscope consists of a spinning wheel mounted on an axle, this axle is held in place by a metal frame; the wheel and the axle spin freely within the frame. While the wheel is spinning the gyroscope's axle it is able to maintain its orientation regardless of the influence of external forces. My family culture acts as my spinning wheel, keeping me upright and on the right path regardless of outside forces.

My family members' accomplishments have had a lasting impact on what I believe I can achieve. Their exploits have raised, and continue to raise, my horizon of aspiration.

Around the time when I was 6 I can recall reading newspaper articles about my brother's exploits on the football field with my dad. My dad, aware of my siblings' influence on me, was always quick to point out that the articles were also constantly mentioning my brother's high GPA and other commendable academic feats. These reading sessions always left me feeling slightly uneasy about the pressure I knew I would be under once I reached high school. However, they also left me feeling empowered, because my siblings constantly told me I could be as good if not better than them. After some time, I believed it.

In my environment I have been introduced to a number of temptations and possible roadblocks. However, standing on the shoulders of my siblings that have come before me has allowed me to experience the benefits of hindsight and avoid their same missteps all while still moving forward.

One situation in which my "spinning wheel" has functioned to near perfection occurred during my freshman year. Before I entered high school, I remember having a conversation with my oldest brother about his high school experience. I asked him if he would have done anything differently and if he regretted anything. After pondering the question for a moment, he replied and told me that he just wished that he had "maintained a better temperament." His answer surprised me because he is one of the most rational and composed people I know. Eager to learn exactly what had happened, I asked him to tell his story in full length. He proceeded to recount how he had been called the n-word by one of his schoolmates, and how they had gotten in an altercation that led to both of them being suspended for two days. I remember thinking to myself how that wasn't too bad of a punishment, until he came to the part about college applications. He told me that while filling out his application for his number one college choice, he came across a question that asked whether he had ever been suspended. In his words "my knees buckled," because he knew his answer to the question would probably bar his entry into his dream school.

My first year in high school began smoothly, I played football and was able to meet a number of my closest friends. However a couple months into my first year I came upon a situation that had the potential to knock me off of the path towards my goals. While walking to my fourth period class I saw one of my "friends." He was with a group of popular kids, most of whom I did not know. I said "Hey look it's T____," to him and he replied with a smirk, "Hey look it's a nigger." This quick exchange was followed by a number of loud "Ooooh's" from the small crowd that had already gathered and was now focused on us two, undoubtedly anticipating a show. Blood rushed to my face and my fists clenched. I was infuriated, and all too ready to react violently. In the split second before I made any move I had a flashback to the conversation I had with my brother the previous summer. I recalled his vivid description of the devastation he felt when he realized that one rash decision he made had shattered his opportunity to attend his dream school. This flashback effectively drained any intention I had of fighting. I turned around and walked to class. Although I felt humiliated, I knew I had acted wisely, and had my brother to thank for my ability to keep my equanimity in that situation. Surprisingly enough, T____ and I are now close friends and have managed to move past this potentially damaging episode.

Being the youngest in my large family has allowed me to gain the numerous benefits of experience without actually having to experience the same testing situations that my older siblings went through. However, when I do stumble into situations with the potential to quickly turn negative my "spinning wheel" allows me to stay balanced and moving forward to my goals.

ANALYSIS

What's really good about this type of essay is that Olutosin successfully portrays strong personal character. What's more, he shows how this character allowed him to rise above adversity, a mark of maturity that is desirable in a Stanford candidate. His method of doing this is particularly thoughtful and well executed. He starts by expressing a strong conviction. This is good because it shows that he's thoughtful and reflects a strong sense of self. Next, he applies a metaphor, and then expounds providing a specific and moving instance of how learning from his family benefitted both his experience and his moral fiber.

Olutosin also gives appropriate credit to his circumstances for his personal success. Generally, people like to take credit for their accomplishments, citing all the toiling and hard work they've invested. There's nothing wrong with receiving credit where it's due (and often it's important to relate an outcome to one's diligence and tenacity), but it takes a lot of wisdom as well as an admirable dose of humility to have enough perspective to see and credit one's inherited advantages. This author was the youngest in a family centered on good values, and he very openly ascribes some amount of his success to his ability to learn from his family members.

The powerful metaphor he uses at the beginning sets a brilliant tone for the essay. The fact that a gyroscope isn't a familiar word to most people subtly implies that the author is well read, and the use of the metaphor itself reflects creativity and writing proficiency. In terms of writing style, the essay reads well, develops interestingly and expresses a lot in relatively little space. There is also a thoughtful reading effect created by the author paralleling an experience with his brother's, and the fact that he handles the situation differently drives home the point of his essay. The title is well chosen and very strong. It really captures the author's point about benefitting from the experiences and guidance of his family, and once again portrays a strong sense of humility.

Overall, this essay is successful for two reasons. First, it's just a good essay: it's well written, it's interesting, it lacks grammatical errors and it implements sophisticated but readable syntax. Second, it illustrates a valuable and stable trait about the author: this one is surprisingly tricky for students to incorporate. Oftentimes the tendency can be to write about something "big" (some big accomplishment, some wild experience) and more often than not those things can be the basis of successful essays. But what's great about this essay is that the specific story (the incident with T____) was just a means to expressing the author's appreciation for how he has benefitted morally and intellectually from his family; this appreciation itself reflected a lot of positive things about the author that made him a successful Stanford applicant.

"Family Photo"

Rolando De La Torre, Jr.

THE PICTURE ENCLOSED IS OF A very small fraction of the most important part of my life- my family. I consider myself very lucky to have been brought up with a huge, extremely close knit family. Much of who I am today is a result of these relatives.

My father is the sixth child of eleven (with this being said, my family is already bigger than most my friend's families.) Next to be considered are my 24 first cousins and my 10 second cousins that have been brought up with me like first cousins. It is impressive to actually think about the dynasty of sorts that my two grandparents began.

I was never lonely as a child. If ever my parents were not around, my siblings and I always stayed with "Tio,"(uncle) "Tia,"(aunt) and "los primos"(the cousins). This always served to our advantage, as it was far easier to invent games to play when there were more players. One of our favorites was "penucho." First of all, nobody remembers where on earth we came up with the name of this game, as the word "penucho" means absolutely nothing in either English or Spanish. Penucho was a wrestling game in which we used to find great amusement, until either somebody got hurt, or some adult intervened. It didn't matter which uncle or aunt was in charge of my brother (as "penuche" emerged in the pre-sister era), my cousins, and me-we would all get punished as if it were mom or dad.

It may be odd that I remember punishment as one of the most important parts of my early days. Perhaps it's because the beauty of it was that I knew that whoever was instituting the punishment still loved me. When I think about it now, I realize how much this affects me today. The notions of discipline and respect were driven in to me early, and remain firmly implanted in who I am. Most important, I think is the fact that I have absolutely no resentment towards those who may have delivered a spanking here or there or a stem reproach to me when I was young.

This picture was taken in about 1998 when we gathered for Christmas at my aunt Rosalinda's house (I am on the bottom left). Many more people were present than the ones shown. A Christmas gathering in my family rivals any family gathering seen in *The Godfather*. If someone were to ask me what I was given for Christmas on a given year, odds are I would not remember. If I was asked about who was there and what we did, I would be able to recall many vivid details. It is praying the Rosary with my grandmother, hugging all of my aunts, listening to my uncles' stories and advice, and being with my cousins that makes Christmas special for me. This is so because of the abundance of amazing people that I have been blessed to have as my relatives.

Many struggles lie ahead of me. As I begin to explore this world on my own and discover new things, many things will change. One thing will always be true. I will always have my family. They will always be there to support me, regardless of the situation. When my grandfather passed away last year his funeral was perhaps the single incident that up to this point in my life has left the strongest impression on me. Every emotion ran through me, but none stronger than the sense of love and unity between each and every member of my family. It struck me hard at this time just how special my situation is. There is nothing I am more proud of than my relatives, and the ability we have to come together and lift each other up, no matter what the crisis is.

I am proud to say I am the son of immigrants who have worked for everything they have. I am a grandson, son, brother, nephew and cousin to the most amazing people in the world. I am blessed with the strong culture and morals that have been instilled in me because of my family. The riches that I have can never be used up or lost. I have chosen to take my life in a positive direction in hopes that one day my family will be as proud of me as I am proud of them.

ANALYSIS

As the author himself notes, this is not a polished essay. He admits some redundancies, some vagueness and the occasional cliché. The essay touches on a multitude of topics: the made-up childhood game of "penucho," Christmas 1998, and the author's grandfather's funeral. But it's clear that the essay has much more to offer: Rolando takes a generally-applicable and fairly universal topic—family—and offers insight on his relationship to his family and how the size and closeness of his family influenced him as he grew up in extremely unconventional and thus memorable ways. For instance, rather than begin with the more typical types of family gatherings at the holidays or in times of sorrow, he starts off describing how he, his brothers and his cousins would be punished for wrestling. The revelation that any adult in his family could punish him as severely and authoritatively as his own parents could, and the realization that he would feel no resentment towards and, in fact, still love the punishing adult shows a remarkably unique way of thinking about ordinary family interactions that most of us would prefer to forget. The author is not only demonstrating how deep his family's bonds run, but he is also showcasing an important ability to spin scenarios positively and to apply general, accepted concepts like unconditional familial love to unconventional and unexpected situations.

It is this ability to frame an otherwise common sentiment in unusual and thoughtful terms (the point, for instance, that Rolando makes about Christmas: he wouldn't remember a single present, but he would remember who was there and what happened) and the conversational, almost confessional tone that wins in this essay, more so than any balanced anecdotal narrative would: the quirkiness of Rolando's family and the silly details—the game "penucho," for instance, reminds nearly every reader of their own ridiculous childhood games—gives a glimpse of the author as a genuine, honest and uniquely reflective person. Nevertheless, Rolando could capitalize further on his ability to recall details by injecting more details into his essay—his reflection on Christmas, when he says, "If I was asked about who was there and what we did, I would be able to recall many vivid details," and then recalls "hugging all of my aunts, listening to my uncles' stories and advice," readers are left wishing they might get to know a few of the aunts by name, or catch a snippet of the uncles' stories and advice—Rolando has set his family up as particularly quirky and unique, and we are left wanting to know more individual details. Similarly, we'd like to know exactly what he means when he says "Much of who I am today is a result of these relatives," or "Many struggles lie ahead of me." What "new things" is he discovering? Rolando might have made more room for these specific details by avoiding occasional redundant comments (he says at the beginning of the essay that the picture shows just a small fraction of his family, and then again in the fifth paragraph states that many more people were present). Nevertheless, it is the honesty and the uniqueness of the essay's formulation of common concepts that is this essay's strongest asset, and to some extent, the unpolished moments enhance the sense that Rolando is holding a conversation with the reader that is frank, from-the-heart, and most of all, genuine.

"What Does Your Dad Do?"

Reade Levinson

"WHAT DOES YOUR DAD DO?" I was watching my bulky suitcase disappear through the flaps of the x-ray machine as the Israeli security guard glared down at me. I glanced up to a pair of overbearing eyebrows and a deep scowl that perfectly matched The Terminator's, and decided quickly that now was probably not the best time to lie that my dad worked in the stock market.

"I don't have a dad," I said, and tried to meet his gaze. He shifted his hefty weight from one combat boot to the other and nodded down at me, suspicious. "I have two moms."

He looked at me blankly. "I have two moms. I don't have a dad." There was a pause. "They're gay."

"Oh, oh!" He blushed slightly, and glanced around him uncomfortably. The Terminator resemblance all but vanished. "But, then, how were you born?"

I took a deep breath and wondered why that always seemed to be the next question, whether it was the boy next to me during sex-ed in fifth grade as we learned about the sperm and egg or the nosy French teacher as I handed in my sheet the first day of school with the 'father' space crossed out. "He's a family friend," never seemed to suffice. Their mouths would hang open long before I'd gotten to the "he's gay too, my mom was a surrogate for one of his kids. Sort of like a trade," part.

"Sperm donor," I finally said, wincing at the massive language barrier that prevented him from understanding. He shrugged and I grabbed my luggage, happy to blow yet another mind with the simple story of my family.

It really is that simple. What may have been trips to Sephora on my thirteenth birthday were replaced with endless shopping sprees at Costco. Instead of a soft-spoken father to teach me carpentry, driving, or mowing the lawn, I had two out-spoken, short-haired, buff moms to teach me the same things.

I can look into any closet in the house and find something to wear, if I'm out of options, although sometimes the overwhelming number of camping shorts and muscle tees sends me scurrying away. I can get relationship advice by the barrelful and we talk freely over family dinners of periods and sex and how men these days never shave.

It no longer unnerves me to be among hundreds of other gay couples, either at San Francisco's gay pride parade or in Maples Pavilion watching a Stanford women's basketball game. I've grown gradually more comfortable, and finally proud, to march annually outside the Sacramento courthouse.

I am lucky to have perspective rarely enjoyed by my friends. My childhood threw me violently outside the box of society and I've learned, slowly, to appreciate that. Some people never get to witness my incredible gay-dar in action or hear me tell stories about my moms. Every once in a while another person finds out, asking, "What does your dad do?" What a long answer that is.

ANALYSIS

Reade's essay shines because she utilizes space efficiently, enfolding drama, providing genuine insight into her life and background and showing her true personality, all within 500 words. Combining dialogue, deftly written descriptions and a bit a humor, Reade's essay reads like an excerpt out of a page-turning novel.

Right from the get-go, she sets the mood by illustrating a situation of peril. Everyone knows that you can't mess around in an airport, and she captures the daredevilish feeling of the moment perfectly with the "glaring" security guard, the "overbearing eyebrows" and the "deep scowl" resembling that of the Terminator's. To boot, she uses some dramatic irony when she shares that she shouldn't lie about her dad's job. Three sentences in and the reader is already wondering what mysterious outcomes the story will provide.

Reade goes on to reveal how she has two moms. She walks us through her thought process and reflections on how people always ask how she was born, and the paragraph-long tangent subsequently builds the suspense of the moment. As we wait to see how she will respond to the security guard, Reade invites us further into her past, recalling the boy in fifth grade and her "nosy French teacher." This gives readers a window into just how long-standing an effect her family situation has had on her.

It is this raw and unpretentious exposure that earns the reader's respect, because Reade shares her story confidently and willingly, even if the situations she describes may have been potentially embarrassing. The reader can see that Reade is unguarded in telling her story, and this makes her seem more likeable.

Reade then shows a bit of her sassy side when she concludes her interaction with the security guard by "shrugging" and walking away, and then acknowledging how she "[blew] yet another mind with the simple story of [her] family." Whether or not the reader likes the sassiness, Reade further establishes her self-confidence.

In the remaining reflective paragraphs of the essay, Reade takes the scenario at the airport and relates it to important life lessons she's learned from her family. She draws parallels between "traditional" parents and her own, showing more of her lighthearted side (calling her moms "buff"), but also revealing a new level of growth. Perhaps the most telling part of the essay is how Reade admits that it "no longer unnerves [her]" to be among gay couples, and that she has "grown gradually more comfortable, and finally proud" to support her moms' and fellow gay couples' rights.

It is this subtle admission—that Reade once struggled with these issues, perhaps throughout childhood—that helps us appreciate how she has grown into the young woman she is today. She can now face the issues and give her support to her family and others despite whatever awkwardness her family may have caused her previously. This is an almost textbook example of the perfect way to tell one's story. No matter what you've been through—trial, triumph, embarrassment, pride or anything in between—the most important message to relay is how you've learned or grown from your experience. Not everyone can claim a family story or childhood like Reade can, but everyone can talk about an experience that taught them an important lesson.

For us, Reade's message feels quite refreshing, because she is willing to share the struggles she went through, and at the same time, she maintains her composure, her wit and her personality. Ultimately, it is her honest and willing portrayal of her past as well as her present thoughts and reflections that make us like her more, and as a result, we are able to feel like we can truly relate to Reade, no matter how similar or different our situations may be from hers.

"The Source of My Being"

Ali Cardenas

TO MANY, LIFE WITHOUT MONEY, MATERIALISTIC items, or even food would appear impossible. I could be a bum whose only possessions include the tattered clothes on my back, yet I would still have the ability to be content. However, if my family were to disappear from my life, especially my parents, my power to smile, to achieve, to perceive, would slowly diminish.

I have always had a close relationship with my family. Even now, with the busy schedule of an involved teenager, I still find the time for them, even if it means going to a younger cousin's *Toy Story* themed birthday party.

Of course, every action I take, every test score I aim to achieve, every field hockey game I strive to win are done to satisfy my own personal aspirations; yet my family is a significant contributor to my actions, behaviors, and thoughts. Both of my parents did not attend college, my brother lost his position at Cal Poly San Luis Obispo, and my sister is currently enrolled in her fifth year of high school. Each time I come home with a flawless report card or spend hours explaining my hectic day, a glimmer appears in their eyes as their white teeth begin to shine before me. Their reaction is what allows me to do so well.

I know that my parents do not expect me to be perfect, nor have they ever, but there is something marvelous that comes with the satisfaction of knowing that I have made them proud. I have heard them bragging to their friends about my grades, my future plans, my ability to excel all while being thoroughly involved in school, and their joy always leaves a great impact upon me.

Since I was young, I considered myself to be extremely self-motivated. The drive that recedes within me has never been fueled by interest in rewards or special treatment. I work hard to satisfy my own needs of achievement. However, if it were not for my parents and the great pride they receive in seeing me exceed, I would not be able to be where I am today.

My family means the world to me.

ANALYSIS

Ali's essay opens with a statement of conviction; she tells us her family is more important to her than shelter, food and material possessions. She tells us it is her close relationship with her family and their pride in her accomplishments that help her stay motivated in her academic and extracurricular pursuits. Ali's writing is earnest and sincere, and although the subject matter of the importance of family may feel familiar, the detail Ali provides gives the essay personality and builds a portrait of her individual character and circumstances.

Details personalize this essay and allow the admissions committee to learn about the particular life of this student. We learn Ali plays field hockey and excels in school. We also learn that neither her parents nor her siblings have completed college. This information about the educational background of her family makes Ali's personal motivation more meaningful. Overall, the positive mood maintained in the writing demonstrates Ali's strength of character and desire to "persevere." This essay takes what could have been a story fixated on adversity and creates a confident view of how strength of character and determination contribute to Ali's accomplishments in an environment where there is a lack of role models for the type of academic successes she has attained.

Because Ali writes that her family's sense of pride in her achievements is as important, if not a more important factor in her achievements, the essay could benefit from an example from her life to support this claim. A meaningful example could bring the impact of familial support on her ability to continue to do well in school to life. This could have been an opportunity for the essay to show how a specific goal was set and achieved and how Ali relied on her family for motivation and drew upon the inner strength her family gives her.

Ali's essay ends with the phrase, "My family means the world to me" but a different ending may be more appropriate because this final sentence states in broad terms the particular ideas already clearly conveyed in the essay and doesn't provide additional insight. Perhaps the essay could end with the previous paragraph's final sentence "... I would not be able to be where I am today." allowing the essay's concluding sentence to focus on Ali and reinforce the nature of her particular academic journey. The ending of an essay should capture the reader's attention as much as the beginning and the middle. Carefully consider your concluding thoughts and summarizing statements. A conclusion that speaks too broadly may weaken an essay's overall impact. It's important to remember that the ending to an essay leaves the reader with a final impression; generalizations or simply restating what the essay has already said doesn't add additional insights or essential information.

"The Fundamental Tracks of Life"

Katherine Christel

DAY 237 AT WORK, AND I am bludgeoned with commands to immediately embark on a record-breaking project—constructing the world's largest railway in order to gain the approval of my dictatorial boss, Matt. Without a minute to take in the absurdity of this challenge, Matt beckons me into what he refers to as the "playroom," the room in which we construct our model train tracks. He then proceeds in pelting me with requirements. His precious project must have bridges so long that they give the Great Wall of China a run for its money. His prized railroad tracks must travel through tunnels so deep within earth's mountains that sunlight will never reach them. His "baby" must be able to walk on water.

After saying goodbye to any potential plans for the night, Matt and I embark on the tedious process of piecing together our model train tracks. Pride swells within our chests as fantasy is made into reality, and our monstrosity of a railway begins to form into a picturesque scene before our eyes. Within the hour, our tracks stretched from one end of the playroom to the other, winding between makeshift cities, dipping into valleys, plowing through mountains, and skating across lakes.

We then turn our attention to the next obstacle ahead of us—getting our massive set of railroad tracks to circle back to the beginning. Luckily the darkening sky provides a welcomed escape, and I inform

Matt that I am off the clock. We retire for the night, Matt drooling over his cherished train tracks, and me feverishly searching for a viable excuse to not return the next day.

Day 239 at work, and I place the final connector piece into our maze of tracks. Matt and I climb onto the couch and allow our transfixed eyes to trace the tracks as our model train weaves throughout the playroom, snaking through plains, climbing over hills, traveling from one country to the next, and at last arriving once again below our feet. Mission accomplished. Matt and I make eye contact, and with his nod of approval, we leap from the couch and begin smashing the model train tracks apart! With a deafening crash, the mammoth-sized bridge is devoured, clattering amongst the debris. Within seconds, we reduce our masterpiece to a hefty pile of overturned wooden tracks and rubble. Our work done for the day, Matt brushes his tiny hands together and moves onto his next challenge—cleaning the playroom before Dad gets home.

Babysitting for Matt has been the most rewarding experience of my life. My soon-to-be little brother has taught me how to be the engineer of my life. He has demonstrated how everything must circle back to the beginning sooner or later. He has instructed me not to invest my entire being into something that could come crashing down at any moment. He has allowed me to live my childhood once more, and through him I will always be able to venture off of the tracks.

ANALYSIS

Katherine's essay is a great answer to anyone who says a babysitting job isn't a resume-builder. She takes what could be considered a pretty ordinary experience, babysitting, and turns it into a thrilling adventure through her powerful writing and playful attitude. She starts with an ingenious hook that plays with readers' expectations. Normally, it's not good for your reader to wonder exactly what is going on in your college essay. In this case, however, Katherine uses a slight sense of confusion and curiosity to great effect, keeping the reader guessing about what's going on until they realize that the "playroom" is, in fact, a playroom.

Not only does Katherine pique the reader's curiosity, but she also creates a successful essay on an aesthetic level. That is to say, it's just plain well written. You might vaguely remember an English teacher imparting to you the importance of vivid verbs. Reading this essay should remove any doubts you had about the power of a good verb. Imagine how much less effective this sentence would be without the vivid verbs: "Within the hour, our tracks *stretched* from one end of the playroom to the other, *winding* between makeshift cities, *dipping* into valleys, *plowing* through mountains, and *skating* across lakes" (italics added). Advanced readers will also notice the list's parallel structure: lovely verb, then preposition, then place noun. Katherine's images are evocative—"tunnels so deep within earth's mountains that sunlight will never reach them," "we reduce our masterpiece to a hefty pile of over-turned wooden tracks and rubble." Not everyone is a lyrical writer, but Katherine is. If you have the talent to pull off a piece like this, by all means choose an essay topic that allows you to showcase your ability. If Katherine had chosen a drier topic or written a more conventional expository or persuasive essay, admissions officers might not have seen her talent for beautiful and imaginative expression.

In Katherine's final paragraph, she outlines the deeper meaning she has gleaned from her time with Matt. Since the bulk of her essay is devoted to a delightful vignette, her decision to make the "big picture" section brief and to-the-point is a wise one. She has already won readers over with her descriptive power, so she doesn't need to beat them over the head with a belabored description of what she learned. Without overdoing it, her succinct statements show the reader that she chose this particular story for a reason and demonstrate just how apt a metaphor the building project is for some important lessons. Finally, her closing line echoes the essay's main motif without sounding cheesy. Few high school students can write at the level that Katherine does—if you are one of them, make the most of the opportunity to show it in your essay.

"Who Are You, He Said, Who Are You"

Sammi Rose Cannold

MY GRANDFATHER ALWAYS USED TO TELL me how I was charming and poised—how I looked like the Polish girls from Kutno back home. He'd stroke my cheek and tell me he was "pyszny," *proud* of what I'd become. Today, he only says, "Who are you?"

The question is disorienting. "Poppa? Remember me, the one who read with you all those years, who played marbles with you—your granddaughter?" Nothing. And while his repeated, "Who are you?" could call for the straightforward answer of, "Sammi," I like to think Poppa wants detail; his loss of memory is my challenge. So I ask the question of myself: who am I, really? I could list superficial characteristics as if for the back of a milk carton: 5'3", dark brown eyes, 17-years-old, often seen wearing bows in her hair and ballet flats on her feet. But I like to think Poppa wants more.

I am a debater, Poppa: quick on my feet, shrewd, and fast-paced in my speech. Sometimes that bothers you—you tell me to slow down. I am obsessed with the Finnish Education System, with international affairs, with global perspectives; I am a policymaker-in-training, ready to change the world, just like you told me I would. I am a relentless risk-taker in chasing my dreams, presenting research to conferences of PhD-holders and editorializing in my school newspaper. The risks go beyond my writing: I started reading Russian literature to get new perspectives and ended up with Chekhov always on my nightstand. I am a lover of philosophy, too—of John Stuart Mill, of Kant, of Nietzsche. My risk-taking drives me to pursue perfection; I am a constant editor, and sometimes that trait makes me too hard on my brother, Noah, when I wish I weren't. I am a leader: running debate practices, holding workshops for my newspaper staff, heading meetings for my school's Parliament. Consequently, I am always busy. I am a snail-mail pen pal to 11 friends worldwide, but I'm rarely on Facebook—no time. I am in a love affair with learning, choosing CNN and NPR for my car rides home and *Jeopardy!* for my DVR. I am driven, singular, and relentlessly curious—excited to see what I will accomplish and ready to knock the socks off the world. But most of all, Poppa, I am your granddaughter, and I am full of a wrenching sadness that you don't seem to remember me.

You used to joke that if I ate an apple a day for 100 years, I'd live a very long time. But I'm going to need an orchard, Poppa; 100 years is not enough for me to accomplish everything I want to. I hope you know that the young woman standing in front of you is more than the one designated to bring you your Jell-O, Poppa. I am Sammi, but I am also much, much more.

ANALYSIS

Half the battle of a college essay is figuring out what you want readers to know about you. The other half is deciding how to distill and convey that information. After all, there is more to each and every person than can be communicated in 500 words or less. One strategy to deal with this constraint is to focus on just one aspect of your personality or one episode in your life, but you run the risk of sounding one-dimensional. Another strategy is to briefly discuss many different facets of who you are, but you run the risk of sounding scattered. Sammi manages to communicate many important parts of herself without losing her focus. The need to identify herself to her grandfather gives the essay a coherent purpose. She bookends the body of her piece, her search for the best way to explain who she is, with charming, old world ways her grandfather has described her. By framing her essay this way, she implicitly shows that she is an empathetic person and a devoted granddaughter, as well as a writer well equipped to deal sensitively with a poignant subject. She maintains this thread by addressing her grandfather by name throughout the essay, making the reader feel as if he or she is listening in on a personal conversation.

Even though the meat of Sammi's essay pulls in a range of examples of what Sammi does—learn about the Finnish Education System, write letters, present research in front of PhD's, avoid Facebook, etc.—she unites them under some umbrella statements about who she is—a risk-taker, a leader and a learner. It is obvious that the examples included here are chosen with care, as each one conveys new information about the author's character. If you're incorporating a wide variety of points like this, follow Sammi's example and make sure that each one adds something to the picture of who you are and that there is no repetition. Sammi also includes some nods to the drawbacks that go along with her strengths, such as her tendency to be too tough on her brother or to speak too quickly for her grandfather to follow. This piece conveys enthusiasm and drive without overstatement—and without the use of buzzwords like "passion" (or, even, "enthusiasm" and "drive"). Because the details of her activities are telling, Sammi doesn't need to do much to emphasize how amazing she is.

9

HERITAGE AND IDENTITY

"China"

Anonymous

A NARROW PATH RAN BETWEEN THE rice paddies an hour outside of Xiamen, a southern city in China. It meandered up a mountain shaded by broad, green leaves. My eccentric and eclectic family trudged along this dirt trail under the blazing summer sun—grandpa and grandma wearing loose traditional Chinese clothing, my mother, brother and me melting in our shorts and t-shirts. We wound our way to the grave, ducking under branches and swatting at gnats that buzzed around our heads. As we plodded into the clearing, we gazed up at the fifty-foot granite slab engraved with scarlet characters that marked the tomb of my mother's grandmother.

By then, my mother had begun to cry, salty tears streaming down her face and dripping from her chin onto the small altar that held a pot of sand for the smoking incense sticks, a faded photograph, and some shriveled, brittle flowers. With reverence and familiarity, she kneeled on the dusty ground, clutching the incense sticks between her hands and bowed three times before the grave. She beckoned my brother and me to join her and handed us each a few smoking sticks. Together, we kneeled and touched our heads to the ground.

I leaned with the incense between my fingers, trying to mimic the smooth grace with which my mother bowed. She burned stacks of feathery paper bills to ensure the wealth of her amah in the afterlife and set off strings of firecrackers to frighten away any demons that threatened her grandmother's soul. Next to her, I stood gasping in the blue-gray smoke from the flames, choking on the overpowering smell of incense.

Watching my mother uproot weeds and dead flowers as she cleaned the gravesite, I realized that although I had felt awkward partaking in the ritual, part of me admired her graceful bows and enjoyed the sickly sweet smell of smoking incense. I had thought there was nothing in common between my mother and me besides appearance; however, I discovered that we are similar beyond our dark, almond-shaped eyes and narrow face, that we shared a heritage and culture, and that we admired the liveliness of Chinese folk music and intricacy of Chinese knotting.

China stepped into the limelight of my life. It was no longer the tedious Chinese homework I was required to do "for my own good" every week; it became an essence residing within me, nurtured by my mother's stories of her youth in the countryside, just waiting for me to realize its existence and to allow it to emerge from its twelve-year-long hibernation. In front of that grave, my mother awoke the Chinese half of me. In spite of my discomfort watching her weep, I learned something on that mountain, something my mother had taught me indirectly, about the Chinese heritage that had gone unnoticed and unappreciated by me. Though I am a Chinese American, I had considered myself only an American before this visit, but since then, I have embraced the Chinese part of my identity—from its complex language and beautiful art to its thousand years of history.

After this trip to China, I volunteered to teach English to Chinese senior citizens thinking that teaching would further develop my Chinese language skills and at the same time fulfill my community service requirement for graduation. During my sophomore year, I took a language proficiency test and received a scholarship to study Chinese language and culture for the summer at the Beijing Normal University, a prestigious university in China. Debarking after an 18-hour trip to China on my own, I was immediately thrust into a completely different world, a world in which I had the opportunity to improve upon a language I knew well, but not fluently. My experiences in China opened my eyes to the beauty of its traditions—from the incense and firecrackers my mother lit at the grave to the eating of sweet moon cakes during the Mid-autumn Festival. I had begun a journey that slowly uncovered the mysteries of China's culture and its determined, hopeful, and compassionate people. With renewed zest, I returned to teaching, more confident in my knowledge of Chinese, excited to share my experiences, and eager to discover more about China from my students.

ANALYSIS

This writer's strengths are immediately apparent: the author's description of the tomb's setting and the path leading up to it are vivid and attentive but at the same time concise, adding color and interest to the essay without dominating it or overpowering the narrative. Details such as the differences in dress between the author and the author's grandparents, the smell of incense and the "feathery paper bills" are striking and memorable, and lead the reader to notice and be enchanted by the same details that the author herself noticed and was enchanted by and that awakened her interest in and led her to engage more actively with her Chinese heritage. The reader's journey through the essay, in a sense, mimics the author's own journey. The author manages to present a lively, beautiful and vivid picture without being too flowery or baroque, and without distracting from the story of her own transformation.

Concision and focus also aid this author outside of her use of descriptive language: the essay is focused around a single experience and its effects. This allows the author to bring in the vivid details that she does, and it also allows her to develop several themes that she returns to throughout the essay: the theme of teaching, for instance, and the contrast between her understanding of her Chinese heritage as existing solely in appearances before her trip, and her Chinese heritage as she lives and participates in it during and after her trip.

The author also sets up a strong opposition between her Chinese heritage as it exists in appearances and her Chinese heritage as it exists in practice, and as she participates in it. Before her trip, the author understood her heritage primarily in appearances and rote activity: in her resemblance to her mother, in her Chinese school homework and her awkward presence at the ritual. With the anecdote of her participation in the ritual at the tomb, the reader sees the author beginning to engage with her Chinese heritage in its practice, in its liveliness and in her living connection to it, through Chinese folk music and knotting, the ritual with its firecrackers and incense at the tomb and the foods associated with the Midautumn festival.

The author also manages to bring in a recurring theme of teaching and learning, communicating both her passion for learning as well as including details about her extracurricular activities and how seamlessly they integrate with one another: the author contrasts the homework she does "for her own good" with the teaching that her mother does implicitly, by telling stories and including the author in rituals, and the effect the different modes of teaching have on the author's own learning and understanding of her heritage. She too takes up the task of teaching—this time teaching English to Chinese senior citizens, but she notes that she, too, is a student in this endeavor, "eager to discover more about China from my students."

"My Lumpy Head"

Anonymous

"DOES THE LUMP ON YOUR HEAD hurt?" I have heard this question countless times throughout my life, as most strangers that I encounter judge me on the basis of my appearance. My hair is waistlength, quite peculiar for a boy. The reason for this is because my Sikh religion requires males to have uncut hair and wear a turban in order to keep their hair orderly and protected, as hair is considered God's gift. As per my Sikh faith, I choose to abide by this tenet and keep my long hair tied up in a bun and knotted by a bandana-like cloth, called a "patka." However, this leaves a 4-5 inch protrusion on my head which is most often the subject of discussion, and unfortunately mockery, by those around me.

As a young child, kids pulled on my hair and mistook me for a girl. Growing up, I was picked on and found myself the last person chosen for partner exercises. My fifth grade teacher once jokingly told the class that I was "mining gold" under my patka, and I was commonly referred to as the "turbanator" in school. These incidents are a painful reminder of how I am treated differently due to my outward appearance. Deep inside I fully understand the reasons why people behave in such a way.

I am indeed different looking, someone who deviates from the norm, and it is the innate nature of man to react with apprehension to something unfamiliar. While even today I am subject to smirks, glares, and the occasional rude remark by strangers, I have come to embrace my uniqueness. It is not a flaw, but rather an essential part of my character and being. I have learned that being a Sikh in America requires the nurturing of a strong inner sense of identity, and this is something that I have gained through becoming an active member of my local Sikh church, called a "Gurdwara."

The Gurdwara is a place where Sikh families congregate and worship at least twice a week, and has become an important meeting place for the Sikh community. At the Gurdwara I have the company of a group of Sikh youth, therefore providing a forum where we can converse about matters affecting our community. I have taken advantage of this opportunity by volunteering as a Youth Advisor, a position which allows me to teach other Sikhs at the Gurdwara about how to tackle problems similar to those I experienced growing up. Reflecting on my own experiences with my youth group has been an enlightening experience. A Sikh boy recently told me how he hates his hair because students pick on him at school, and I felt great pride sharing my insights to help nurture him as a diverse and special individual. I know that my participation as a youth volunteer is beneficial for not only me to reflect on my challenges but also for the children because they finally have someone to whom they can relate. I help them understand that keeping hair, as a tenet of their faith, is a personal decision.

I am proud that we are able to acknowledge contemporary issues and provide an arena where stories can be shared, ideas can be expressed, and resolutions can be made so as to inspire Sikhs like myself to press forward in life amidst adversity. The prejudice I have encountered as a result of being different has molded me into a stronger, more resilient person. When I am older I will wear a turban like my father and grandfather, and hope my children will carry on this tradition. I wholeheartedly accept that with this decision I will face numerous challenges and a multitude of questions regarding my patka. However, I am confident that I will persevere through these future obstacles in the same manner by which I anticipate conquering the rigors of college.

ANALYSIS

This type of essay topic is very successful for a handful of reasons: it reflects how the author can contribute to the school's community by providing a unique cultural perspective, it displays the author's strength of character in the face of adversity, and it shows that the author is thoughtful and reflective in analyzing how his experiences have shaped his current self. In addition, it describes a touching story about the author becoming truly comfortable in his skin and discusses how he's actively giving back to his community.

In the essay, the author cites and describes how his experiences motivated him to get involved in a cause and take on a leadership position. Taking active roles in one's community is a very desirable trait in a strong candidate, and his sense that doing so not only helps his youth advisees, but also himself is a very insightful remark reflecting his thoughtfulness. What's really strong about how he ends the essay is that he expands the issue further than himself. Even though he starts off speaking specifically about jabs at his personal appearance, and how that appearance is linked to his religion and cultural community, what he says he likes about his place of worship is that they can "acknowledge contemporary issues and provide an arena where stories can be shared, ideas can be expressed." What is expressed is that the author isn't just upset or holding a personal grudge that people say rude and thoughtless things about him. Instead, he's interested in taking a stance socially and intellectually. He is personally involved so that he can take initiative and some authority concerning the issues and adversity that people in his community must face.

Stylistically, the essay works because it is simple. He's telling a story in this essay, so he does just that without filling it with needlessly complicated syntax or verbose run-ons. He successfully hooks the reader with the quote at the opening, and then goes on to describe how this quote has been a constant in his life and what he's done to cope with that personally, as well as reach out and help others facing that same adversity.

All in all, this essay is successful because it portrays the author as someone who is proactive, who takes initiative and leadership in his community. It also reflects that he is passionate and intellectual, and someone who has a well of important experiences to draw from and contribute to his college community.

10

HUMOR

"Roomie Poetry"

Inès C. Gérard-Ursin

Essay prompt: A note to your future roommate

DEAR FUTURE ROOMMATE:
  What you should know about me, is that;
  My friends tell me I snore—or I laugh—or I walk
  or I don't really wake up, and I talk to the clock.
  In any case, I am not sure, I am never awake
  to catch myself making any social mistake.
  When I do wake up, I can be a pain
  and spend ages in the bathroom, or just not be too vain.
  Certain mornings you will hear me doing jumping jacks at five
  or wait, not that early, yet latest at nine.
  But I do tend to scatter all my belongings on the floor
  putting them in their right place can be such a bore.
  Especially when I'm busy, but darling, when I'm not
  be sure to keep all of your desk drawers locked

and your earplugs pushed in, to their maximum extent
because when I clean, the term "spotless" I reinvent.
Yet I am fairly laid back, you can do what you want
After all, how many years is it until we find another spot?
However, I warn you, with curfews and all
You will find that I can throw quite a few curveballs
and come home at 7, or 11, or 2
I might stay up and chat, or just not see you.
But I can't wait for a roommate, I really enjoy
A constant companion, and we can talk about boys!
Then when we work, my dear, please hold that thought
I am able to concentrate, but with love, and politics, I cannot
On that note, while working I can take a great deal
Of noise, even if they are high-pitched squeals.
So be reassured and comforted my soon-to-be roomie
I am easygoing, hardworking, and boundary-free
And hope you'll have a pleasant time living with me!

ANALYSIS

Inès takes something of a risk by doing the unexpected with her response: writing poetry where ordinarily the admissions officer would expect prose. In this case, since the prompt asks for a more light-hearted task—to write to your future roommate—her writer's choice to be more whimsical than formal is fitting.

The overall effect of this poetic response is that we can tell Inès is having fun with her topic. She expresses a multitude of feelings in a small amount of space, from confusion at her own actions—"In any case, I am not sure, I am never awake / to catch myself making any social mistake"—to self-deprecation—"When I do wake up, I can be a pain"—to pride in her quirky habits—"But I do tend to scatter all my belongings on the floor / putting them in their right place can be such a bore." She even cites the outrageous—"doing jumping jacks at five"—before correcting herself in the next breath—"or wait, not that early, yet latest at nine."

Because she chooses to write a poem comprised of couplets, the structure of the piece allows for humor or drama that a straightforward essay might not provide. For example, seeing how the writer will succeed in rhyming with "extent" or checking how well she keeps in meter can be fun tasks for the reader. Each pair of lines works as a unit, introducing a new thought or action that helps the reader pace through the poem. Along with this pacing comes a feeling of familiarity and comfort as the reader can be assured that issues raised in the first line of each couplet will be resolved in the second line. We also know that given this format, the writer spent a good amount of effort with her word choice and making the poem flow well.

It is for these reasons that this poem as an essay works. While it may seem that writing a poem can be just a flippant response to an essay prompt, in this case, upon further examination we can tell that the writer spent a lot of time constructing her piece, perhaps taking much longer than it would have taken to write a traditional essay.

Regarding this choice to write a poem, Inès certainly took a risk, but it was no doubt a calculated one. It is almost certain that she had to feel quite confident in her ability to take on the poetic form. This is not to say that you should think of all of your essays in terms of how you can take the biggest risk, or that you should never take a risk at all. In some cases, as in lighter prompts like this one, taking a risk may seem appropriate. But risk doesn't have to be changing the format of your response from an essay to a poem. Risk can simply be saying something unexpected, describing something in an expected way or giving the reader an unexpected ending. Even still, you may find that you don't need to take a "risk" at all.

The big message is that you should find the medium or voice that lets you express yourself and your uniqueness in the way you feel most comfortable. Perhaps poetry works for you; if so, then by all means go for it. But perhaps you will be better served telling a story using lots of dialogue, or writing a character sketch or describing an object with no dialogue at all. There is no right or wrong answer when it comes to the "perfect" method to respond to an essay prompt. Simply choose what works best for you.

"Pardon My Puns"

Elena Musz

Essay prompt: A note to your future roommate

DEAR ROOMMATE,

I mulled over what to write you for a while, but in the end realized that no matter how hard I push the envelope, it will still be stationery. Well, there you have it: one of my favorite lame puns. You will be hearing a lot of those, so I figured I would take this opportunity to warn you about my love for exploring language.

I journal frequently, I give fourteen off-the-cuff speeches on most school weekends, and I spend too much time contemplating grammar issues on online linguistic forums. I like to twist terms into my vocabulary and own my words the way some people own socks; I pull them out of a messy [mental] drawer and match them with a nearby mate. I explore word combinations, attempt assonance and make paradoxical puns. I know it is nerdy, but I cannot even tell you how much I enjoy reading masterfully employed literary devices. (Aporia, anyone?) I figured you should know about this passion, because just as words clutter my mind, they will likely clutter our living space (along with the aforementioned mismatched socks).

My room is currently a collection of letters, books, magazines, and performing arts programs. I surround myself with words that inspire me to be creative and remind me of my favorite memories. For this reason, I apologize for when my side of the room becomes littered with literature. You'll probably recognize my love for the humanities though my dorm décor and my campus involvement. One night, I will likely gush to you about the powerful monologues I witnessed in the latest STAMP production and tell you all about my first time going to an event for the Center for the Study of the Novel's Undergrad Colloquia. From there, I might get excited about the potential points "colloquia" could produce on a triple word score and invite you to a game of Scrabble. Of course, if you would rather do something else, we could always have some fun and write a theatrical production about puns. It would be a play on words.

See you soon!
Elena

ANALYSIS

Elena's letter to her roommate examines her unique hobby, experimenting with words. This interest is intriguing and although Elena's first sentence is a bit corny, over the course of the letter we learn to admire Elena's passion for puns.

Overall, the essay both allows us to see Elena's mastery of language and understand how it affects her life. Her second paragraph details what she does — "I journal frequently, I give fourteen off-the-cuff speeches on most school weekends, and I spend too much time contemplating grammar issues on online linguistic forums" — in order to explore language outside of school. These activities show the breadth of Elena's commitment to her interests. Her journaling hobby is a personal way to experiment with words, while online linguistic forums are a social way to learn more about language. These details help us understand how thoroughly Elena's love of language is integrated into her life.

The essay also demonstrates how Elena's experiences with exploring language affect her writing style. Elena carefully integrates many literary devices including alliteration ("paradoxical puns"), metaphor ("own my words the way some people own socks"), pun ("play on words") and aporia ("I cannot even tell you how much I enjoy reading masterfully employed literary devices") into her writing. Although the extensive use of these devices throughout the essay is a bit overdone and obvious, it clearly exhibits Elena's thorough knowledge of the English language. Her use of pun for example, could afford to be subtler. Still, the pervasiveness of pun in Elena's essay attests to the extent of her enthusiasm.

The final paragraph illustrates how Elena plans to continue her zeal for language during college. The description of a dorm room "littered with literature" including "letters, books, magazines, and performing arts programs" gives the reader an image of how Elena will make language a tangible aspect of her future life. Furthermore, Elena predicts building off her current passions by becoming involved with STAMP and the Center for the Study of the Novel's Undergrad Colloquia at Stanford. Mentioning these two lesser-known student groups, which are unique to Stanford, shows that Elena has both researched Stanford and considered how her passion for working with words will contribute to the already vibrant intellectual communities on campus. Elena thus confirms that she has carefully considered why Stanford specifically is a good fit for her.

Finally, Elena brings the essay back to what it really is, a letter to her future roommate. The invitation to play a game of Scrabble reminds us that Elena is talking to one of her prospective peers. We finally see that Elena's devotion to words does not steer her away from her willingness to share her interests and engage with other students. Instead, she encourages her new roommate to play a game, write a play and embrace Elena's love of language.

11

AN INFLUENTIAL PERSON

"Granny"

Sumaya Quillian

Essay prompt: What matters to you, and why?

I NEVER KNEW MY GREAT-GRANDMOTHER, WHOM my family and I refer to as Granny. Loula Quillian passed away when my dad was still in junior high school, but she has always inspired a sense of integrity in me. In the top drawer of my dresser, I have a picture of her circa the 1940s. The photograph is small, but I can clearly see Granny walking down the street in a flower printed dress with her head held high. I have always thought of Granny as a kind of June Cleaver; doing chores in a nice housedress with her hair and make-up done. To this day, my dad talks about the food she cooked, her legendary sauerbraten in particular. My grandpa tells me how proper she was and how much she knew about manners.

I look at her pictures and think how much I hope I will be something like her, a symbol of dignity, strength, and femininity. She was a proud woman. I know because every story I have heard about her and every picture I have seen of her have shown me so. I do not believe that pride is arrogance. Pride is having self-respect and being willing to grow to become a better human being. I try to emulate Granny in so many ways, big and small. Before I go out, I may pick out a bracelet to wear so I look more presentable. I have a strong sense of morality and I support my beliefs, because I realize I have no excuse not to have pride or self-respect. Granny always did, even though as a black woman with little education living in segregated St. Louis, no one expected her to. She knew, without anyone to teach her, that it makes a difference to take pride in the smallest things. That is something I always reflect on. If my family has guests and I am supposed to set cookies out for everyone, I take a moment to find a nice tray and doilies for them. Although food is something I could throw on any plate, I remind myself that presentation matters and "Yes, this is how Granny would have done it." She would have taken time to make simple things look beautiful, and I try my best to do the same.

ANALYSIS

What is most incredible about this essay is the wonderfully expressive and detailed portrait that Sumaya paints of her "Granny"—without even having known her. Sumaya does a number of things here that show off not only her skill as a writer, but her imagination, her strong connection to her family and her self-awareness and values. The portrait of her great-grandmother is wonderfully rich and evocative: from the simple facts that her parents make known, about her cooking and sauerbraten, her life in segregated St. Louis and her manners to the pieces that Sumaya imagines and illustrates from the pictures of her: her nice housedress and makeup, her head held high and her morality, pride and self-respect. Sumaya's imagination and her values come through loud and clear in this essay, and she always takes time to excavate, to ask and answer the question of where these values come from instead of making empty claims. "She was a proud woman. I know because every story I have heard about her and every picture I have seen of her have shown me so. I do not believe that pride is arrogance. Pride is having self-respect and being willing to grow to become a better human being." Sumaya makes it clear that she draws her definition of pride and the pride she tries to take in herself from the example of her grandmother, both from the stories she has heard and notionally, from the image Sumaya has constructed.

The strong unacknowledged current that Sumaya also sets up in this essay is her connection to the rest of her family: it is clear how important her family is to Sumaya, and how close a connection they have to one another—so close that, even without knowing her Granny, Sumaya can feel that she knows her. It would be far too much to cram into a single short essay to say that, but Sumaya shows is in the very best way, letting the reader understand the closeness of Sumaya's family atmosphere and understand that her connection to her Granny is simply one manifestation of that tight-knit relationship.

Finally, Sumaya wonderfully summarizes the lessons she has drawn from trying to piece together her Granny's character and to emulate it: she states the values she believes her Granny embodied, how she knows that her Granny succeeded in them, and the ways in which she tries to apply them to her own life: "Before I go out, I may pick out a bracelet to wear so I look more presentable… She knew, without anyone to teach her, that it makes a difference to take pride in the smallest things. That is something I always reflect on. If my family has guests and I am supposed to set cookies out for everyone, I take a moment to find a nice tray and doilies for them. Although food is something I could throw on any plate, I remind myself that presentation matters and 'Yes, this is how Granny would have done it.' She would have taken time to make simple things look beautiful, and I try my best to do the same." Sumaya's account of her own behavior, ingeniously, mirrors the way that Sumaya discovered her Granny—the same details, the bracelet, the doilies on the plate, the cookies, all might be details in the same kinds of photographs and stories that Sumaya has heard about her own Granny from her own parents, that one day Sumaya's own great-grandchildren might piece together about her.

"The Singing Grandmother"

Kristy Wentzel

"YOU SAY TOMATO AND I SAY to-mato, you say potato…" my grandmother warbled on, oblivious to my sisters plugging their ears.

"Bebe, if you sing one more time, I am going to THROW UP!" my six-year old sister Amy exclaimed. She was a fiery redhead, always one to speak her mind.

My grandmother Bebe loved to sing, to the point that her obsession became annoying. One could be having a normal conversation with her and she would suddenly burst out into a song about one of the words in the conversation. Her latest outbreak occurred when I asked if we could have tomatoes for dinner, and off she went.

"Bebe you have to stop, I mean I love you but you are giving me a headache," my sweet sister Carrie pleaded, hopelessly trying to quiet my grandmother.

"L is for the way you look at me! O is for the only one I see" Bebe started up, switching songs as easily as turning on a light switch.

"Oh, for the love of god, I am going to bed," I declared, giving my adorable grandmother a kiss on the forehead.

At sixty-six, Bebe had the energy of a teenager. She loved going to amusement parks, and shopping for bright outfits. Visiting my grandmother was always an adventure and something that my sisters and I greatly looked forward to. We could always expect a trip to Sea World, wild blueberry picking, and a new outfit from the mall.

This was all two years ago. Recently, Bebe was diagnosed with pancreatic cancer. As my family drove down to see her, I wondered how she would overcome it. I imagined a gaunt, depressed woman, completely different from the grandmother I grew up with. As my family quietly filed into her house at midnight, being careful not to wake her, I was prayed that when I rose the next morning, my loving Bebe had not changed.

"Wakey Wakey! Eggs and Backey!" Bebe sang at the top of her lungs bright and early, throwing open the curtains to expose the sunlight.

"Sleepy head get up!" Bebe shouted, lightly smacking my back. "Oh what a beautiful morning! Oh what a beautiful day!"

My first reaction was to curl up my toes in pure annoyance and shut my eyes tightly. The feeling passed quickly when I realized where I was. I sprang from my bed and surveyed my grandma, whom despite a thinner frame and hair loss, looked just as I remembered, clad in an outrageous pink bathrobe.

"Bebe!" I squealed, wrapping my grandmother in a hug. "It's so good to see you."

"It's good to see you too love. Now come on, help me wake up the rest of this lazy household and then I need to go put some make-up on this decrepit face." As I watched my grandmother pad down the hallway in her bunny-eared slippers, singing, "In the morning when I wake up, before I put on my make-up…" I realized she would always be the same. Nothing, not even cancer, could bring Bebe's spirits down.

Whenever I am overwhelmed with schoolwork, or upset over a bad crew practice, my grandmother comes to mind. Despite her pain, Bebe remains optimistic and light-hearted; always singing as though nothing is wrong. It is her spirit that makes my grandmother, Bebe, my inspiration and her buoyant attitude influences all that I do.

ANALYSIS

The subject of Kristy's essay is her grandmother, Bebe, a lively and upbeat woman with the eccentric habit of seguing from snippets of conversation into classic song tunes. The essay begins with Bebe singing the lyrics, "'You say tomato and I say to-mato, you say pota-to...'" setting a lighthearted tone for the essay. This essay dramatizes the time Kristy spends with Bebe and lovingly bemoans her eccentricities. The essay establishes the close ties and fun that Kristy and her sisters have with her grandmother "going to Sea World, wild blueberry picking, and a new outfit from the mall." And, the essay illustrates the importance and constancy of the relationship with Bebe in Kristy's life.

Kristy accomplishes an active writing style through precise diction, imagery and dynamic sentence structure. When providing details in an essay, the choice of verbs and nouns are just as, if not more important than, the choice of adjectives and adverbs to create an engaging and exciting piece of writing. Effective diction in Kristy's essay is often conveyed in verb choices: "warbled," "pleaded," "sang," "shouted," "surveyed" and "sprang" are more impactful than more common verbs such as said or did. Simile and imagistic language help to enrich the writing: "Bebe started up, switching songs as easily as turning on a light switch" and "...my grandma, whom despite a thinner frame and hair loss, looked just as I remembered, clad in an outrageous pink bathrobe." In addition, Kristy varies her sentence structure and sentence length to keep the pace of the writing moving; for example, in paragraph 8: "This was all two years ago. Recently, Bebe was diagnosed with pancreatic cancer." are two short declarative sentences that begin the paragraph, and the paragraph ends with a multi-claused sentence combining narrative and emotion: "As my family quietly filed into her house at midnight, being careful not to wake her, I prayed that when I rose the next morning, my loving Bebe had not changed."

The lighthearted tone established in the first half of the essay is disrupted when the writer reveals in the middle of the essay that Bebe has pancreatic cancer. The speaker worries her grandmother will have changed, will have lost her vivacious spirit, but it turns out that it's the grandmother's ability to retain her positive outlook and energy that impresses Kristy the most. She realizes her grandmother is a role model for her life because she can maintain an upbeat attitude even in the face of a major illness. Kristy is able to borrow strength from her grandmother's example and handle her own stresses and disappointments in school and her activities.

Kristy presents a loving and heartfelt portrait of her grandmother as a role model that is personal and interesting, but what makes this essay stand out is the quality of the writing. Kristy's writing is active, fluid and lively, demonstrating her ability to organize her thoughts and express herself in words clearly and concisely.

12

ISSUES

"Solving the Omnivore's Dilemma"

Vienna Harvey

Essay prompt: What matters to you, and why?

SOME OF MY EARLIEST MEMORIES ARE of trips to a local farm, picking basil, blueberries or corn depending on the season. These outings were just fun afternoons with my family. It was not until years later that I came to appreciate their significance.

When I read *The Omnivore's Dilemma* at age 12, I learned that modern agriculture relies on a trinity of monoculture, synthetic fertilizers and chemical pesticides. Genetically modified crops are the latest strategy for increasing yields. These methods are exported to the developing world as the only viable solution for feeding the global population, despite the costs: deforestation, water pollution, soil erosion and nutrient depletion. Reading this marked the start of my local-food campaign. At first, I just encouraged my parents to buy organic produce, join a CSA and start a garden.

Since then I have planted heirloom vegetables, studied square-foot gardening and amended our soil with compost from a backyard worm bin. I continue to learn about the "locavore" movement.

As I grow healthy food for my family, I find myself thinking about the implications of how we, all 7 billion of us, might feed ourselves in sustainable ways. Food security means having sufficient, safe and nutritious food. 18.2% of the US population reported not having enough money to buy food in the past year. Approximately 76 million people in the country are sickened by food-borne illness annually. Rates of diabetes and obesity are on the rise. Clearly, our food supply is anything but secure.

Alternatives do exist. Studies show that small farms growing diverse crops provide equal yields when correctly managed. I would argue that a modern version of sustainable, small-scale farming could bring global food security. In this era of economic recession, climate change and international terrorism, food security does not top most people's list of major concerns. To my mind, however, it is a vital issue that we must tackle as a national priority.

ANALYSIS

Vienna's essay "Solving the Omnivore's Dilemma" elegantly illustrates the challenges of the "What matters to you and why?" prompt, as the "what" can easily overwhelm the "you" and "why". People can be very passionate about their principle cause, and, when writing, allow the issue to eclipse the actual subject of the essay: you. Vienna's essay does a good job of balancing information about her important issue—sustainable local agriculture—with anecdotes that illuminate aspects of herself and how the issue plays such a central role in her life.

She begins by grounding the essay in an image of family trips to the local farm, which both sets the scene for the essay but also alludes to a supportive family environment (they take the trips together) as well as an appreciation of educational opportunities outside of the classroom.

Her next paragraph, on the impact of reading *The Omnivore's Dilemma,* is a bit confusing, as she posits positions without value judgment: it's not until she states that reading the book was the beginning of her "local-food campaign" that she has taken a stand against genetically-modified crops and synthetic fertilizers. Don't assume that the reader has the same understanding of the issue or the same values as yourself: explain why *you* dislike chemical pesticides or GM foods and write out that a CSA is a Community-Supported Agriculture and not the Confederate States of America.

Citing "square-foot gardening" and "backyard worm bins" brings the writing back to the writer and implies that she has spent time, thought and effort to actively put position into practice. The following paragraph, citing statistics and facts about the effects of "food security," show that she's done her homework and expanded her awareness of the issue far beyond herself and her family.

"Our Most Inexhaustible Source of Magic"

Cristina H. Mezgravis

Essay prompt: An intellectually engaging idea or experience

"WHAT IS MORE POWERFUL: WORDS OR actions?" I asked as I smiled at my fourteen year old brother's troubled face from across the dinner table.

He set his fork down against the plate, and answered as if it was the most absurd question he had ever heard, "Actions."

"Words," I challenged immediately after this had left his mouth.

He looked at me as if I had three eyes, "If I punched you down it would cause more damage than if I insulted you."

"Maybe your insult would lead to depression and eventual suicide," I replied. We tossed arguments back and forth at each other: six million dead during World War II vs. the Nazi leaders had an effective method of speech that brainwashed the masses; words, if not followed by action, are meaningless vs. words don't need action to have a potential effect, and on we went. Throughout our discussion, our juror had been chewing thoughtfully at the end of the table, until he realized we were both waiting for his verdict.

He took his time savoring the peas in his mouth but finally concluded, "Both are important." Our shoulders dropped the tension they had been carrying as we laughed at his predictability. That answer didn't quench my thirst; I started analyzing every important event in history that popped into my head for how words had played an instrumental part in its outcome.

Two months later at a movie premiere, we watched Albus Dumbledore settle the score for us, "Words are, in my not-so-humble opinion, our most inexhaustible source of magic, capable of both inflicting injury and remedying it." I peeked at my brother from the corner of my eye and found him peeking back at me; he quickly turned back to stare at the screen as soon as I caught him.

I leaned towards him and lightly poked my elbow into his ribs and whispered, "Told ya." Who could argue with the intellectual vitality of a 150 year-old wizard?

ANALYSIS

In this essay the writer uses the playful sequence of a sibling rivalry as the backdrop for a more serious debate. In so doing, she demonstrates her capacity for analytical thought as well as a likable penchant for not taking herself too seriously.

To more effectively tell her story, Cristina employs dialogue as a main vehicle for the essay. Dialogue opens the story and accompanies every step taken in the story's plot; for example, an early turning point in the story occurs when the all important "juror" declares, "Both are important" as his verdict, while later in the essay the writer quotes Dumbledore's dialogue from the movie to verify her argument. By including these quotes, the writer is able to truly share her unique perspective of her experience. The story is made real because the words that the characters speak bring them to life. Dialogue adds excitement to the story and offers readers something they can relate to, as opposed to wordy descriptions or analysis that can become dull or less relatable.

Where dialogue is the primary vehicle for this essay, narration dutifully lays the road for the plot to move forward. Following or preceding every quotation mark is a description or thought directly from Cristina's mind that pushes the story forward—for example, "He set his fork down against the plate, and answered as if it was the most absurd question he had ever heard, 'Actions.'" The narration guides the reader from one step to the next and keeps the story interesting by creating suspense; one example is when the writer builds up the tension of arguing with her brother and she describes how "our juror had been chewing thoughtfully at the end of the table, until he realized we were both waiting for his verdict."

Also notable in the essay is the way in which Cristina touches upon more serious issues, like contemplating the events of World War II and Nazi Germany, as well as "every important event in history," while maintaining a lighter tone overall. Because of this lighter tone, it seems appropriate that she doesn't dwell on these topics, but by describing her meticulous nature of cycling through her thoughts, by sharing that "[t]hat answer didn't quench [her] thirst," she reveals to the reader a bit of her mind's ambition and persistence. These sprinkled moments of seriousness show that, while the writer has a knack for humor, she also shows her capacity for mulling over things properly when it's time for business.

One final comment is that the writer's effective use of humor and colloquial language helps her speak to the reader at his or her level. From the image of having "three eyes" to the vernacular "Told ya" that concludes the story, the writer demonstrates her confidence and comfort with engaging her reader. She doesn't think twice about including slang spelling or fantastic imagery, and as a result, she comes off as having a strong voice.

The humor, real-life dialogue and simplicity of this essay are what make it so easy to read. The character traits the writer reveals about herself and her tactful mention of intellectual pursuits are what make the reader (and admissions officers) believe she is an engaging person worthy of attention.

"What Matters Most"

Anonymous

Essay prompt: What matters to you, and why?

MANY ASPECTS OF LIFE MATTER TO me, from broad social and political issues to pieces of daily living. Beyond family, friends, and the necessities of quotidian existence, nurturing my ability to do well for the world is far and away more important to me than anything else. Of the elements that collectively define me as a person, my sociopolitical beliefs shape my outlook, personality, and personal choices more than anything else.

No issue is of more importance to me than the factory farm system. In factory farms, most animals are not given even the space to turn around. They are forced to wallow in their own excrement, and should they develop an illness, as is common given their close confines and unsanitary environments, they are left to die. The worth of factory farm animals is estimated by their monetary value; their suffering is ignored so long as it does not lessen their value. Making food choices in protest of this system and this mentality is the simplest and most effective means of combating them.

Other issues of great importance to me include gender equality and conservation. I consider myself gender blind. I neither take actions personally out of consideration of gender roles, nor do I project gender roles onto others. I make a constant concerted effort to use as few resources as possible, whether by parking close to my house and walking much of the way to my classes or by reusing virtually everything that I buy. In daily living and in my perceptions, both of these issues play a vital role in my life.

Family and friends are inevitably important, and I try to be as positive a presence in my loved ones' lives as possible. However, my sociopolitical beliefs and the decisions that I make as a result of them are what I hope will leave some lasting impact on the world. To measure the meaningfulness of my life, I can use no scale but that which measures what I have done for others. As a result, my moral stances will always hold the largest space in my value system.

ANALYSIS

Universities know that a major aspect of a great education is having a diverse student population and so they try to cultivate a class comprised of people from all walks of life and with a variety of interests and strengths beyond the purely academic. But even if you're a stellar athlete or math magician, you still need to be able to show you can write a competent, structured essay that directly addresses the topic given.

"What Matters Most" to this student?

The inhumane conditions of the factory farm system, gender equality, conservation, family and friends. All worthy and important.

Each paragraph addresses an important topic or two, and then gives reasons why these are important topics. You can see the structured outline behind the writing which indicates a thoughtful, organized mind.

But what do we know about the *person* who wrote the essay?

We know she has a family and friends and that she cares for animals. We know she can write an essay with paragraphs structured with a topic sentence and some supporting details, so she'll be able to complete college coursework. She has touched on numerous topics, but as the reader we want to learn more about her.

The essay could benefit by having sensory and concrete details, an anecdote or examples, a bit of humor that would help show some more of the person behind the page as well as illuminate how the issues are tied in with her personal experiences and how that's shaped the person she's become. *Why* does she write about factory farming? *Why* is the topic so important to her? Did she grow up on a farm and cared for animals in the way they should? Was she raised in the city and never questioned how her food got on her table until she took a trip or saw a documentary? What "food choices in protest of this system" does *she* make, and how did that affect her mind, her family, her health, her goals? Is there a specific program at Stanford that can help her reach these goals?

The writer finishes her essay with a very strong statement: "To measure the meaningfulness of my life, I can use no scale but that which measures what I have done for others." Thematically she connects her caring for the animals with her love for people and reinforces her message that she has a great desire to give and to help. However, the reader is left with questions: What *have* you done for others? What *will* you do for others? And how can Stanford help? We'd like to learn more about the writer as a person.

"Prejudice Matters"

Anuj Patel

Essay prompt: What matters to you, and why?

IN THE BHAGAVAD GITA, LORD KRISHNA says, "To the illumined man or woman, a clod of dirt, a stone, and gold are the same." In the world today, there are so many stereotypes and prejudices against people who look, speak, and act differently. "Normal" people see fit to act/think differently toward these other people—who are human, just like you and me. One of the prejudices that irks me the most is against those that are mentally challenged. Why should we look upon those people differently? They are also humans. I have an autistic cousin who has trouble interacting and expressing his emotions, but with me, he can say anything. This young boy is the most brilliant, observant, and caring individual I have ever known. There is never a day when he does not call me asking how my day was and how everyone in my entire family is doing. I have the privilege of working with him twice a week, and the time that we spend together is the most meaningful and exciting part of my week. What kills me inside is that at school, he is taunted, excluded, and prevented from participating in many things that common children are involved in because he is autistic and "weird."

I have tried to change people's mindset about these special individuals, only to understand that people are not ready to change. Therefore, I have realized that the only way to change the way people think is through a physical display of character. Every week, in addition to meeting with my cousin, I help coach a youth soccer team for kids with

Down Syndrome. That team is more fun than any sports team I have played on. In addition, during this upcoming summer I will be doing Autism research at Oregon Health and Science University. I am trying to change myself so that others can change themselves. I sincerely hope that one day we can eliminate these prejudices among us. So what matters to me? Doing what I can to show others that these people with disabilities are just as special, unique and intelligent as you and me.

ANALYSIS

Anuj begins his essay by discussing a global issue that matters to him, prejudice. His opening statements are very generic, pointing out how senseless prejudice is in any form. This start does much, because it's so banal. The main point of a college essay is to tell the reader about you as an individual. Any student applying to college could have written the first part of this essay. The distinguishing factor comes in when Anuj gives us his personal insight as to why prejudice is important to him specifically; his autistic cousin helped him see first-hand the evils of stereotyping.

Note that Anuj was not the victim here, or even the main subject of the essay. Still, Anuj is able to tell us a lot about himself by discussing the obstacles that face his cousin. Anuj's ability to see how unjustified bullying and exclusion affects autistic children proves the extent of Anuj's maturity. Even though he was not personally hurt by the other children's actions, Anuj was hurt by the way they affected someone important to him. This show of empathy attests to Anuj's personal character. In addition, Anuj was observant enough to see how even with autism, his cousin shows interest in other people. For example, Anuj points out that his cousin "can say anything" in front of him, and is constantly inquiring about the well being of his family. In this way, Anuj discusses specifically how his cousin is able to relate well to people, even though he might come off as "weird." Again, the reader commends Anuj for his ability to see positive personal qualities in someone others cannot relate to. Furthermore, by humanizing his cousin, the reader is able to relate to him and thus fully realize the injustice that the young boy faces. In turn, we come to understand why prejudice in general bothers Anuj so much.

One of the best parts of this essay is how it develops in the second half. Anuj does not cease after explaining why prejudice matters to him. He goes one step further and talks about what he is willing to do in order to challenge prejudice against mentally challenged youth. He strategically points out that he became a coach for a soccer team for children with Down Syndrome both to do well by those children, and to prove to prejudiced people that children with Down Syndrome deserve the same treatment as everyone else. In this way, Anuj is able to show how he is a leader, willing to take action instead of passively complaining about a problem he sees in his community. This show of character is further solidified by Anuj's declaration to pursue autism research at Oregon Health and Science University. In this way, Anuj proves that he has ongoing commitment to fighting injustice by becoming more involved in his community and in academia. Furthermore, he proves that challenging prejudice truly matters to him.

13

LEADERSHIP

"The Prius of My Class"

Anonymous

I AM THE PRIUS OF MY class. I am efficient, burning with energy, a friend to the environment, and I go the distance. But I am not your basic package, I come fully loaded including the hard to find options of compassion and leadership. When I come to college, I will bring this boundless force of positive energy with me, I will get things done. My compassion for others and leadership skills are the building blocks I use to bring individuals together to complete tasks. I needed these skills when I had to deal with a kindergartener who was also fully loaded.

Imagine being outside on a gorgeous day. The sun is shining, flowers are in their brightest colors, and an odious smell is in the air. This is not a story about a superior smelling skill or how a bad scent can ruin a day; instead it is about taking a compassionate leadership role to keep him part of a community. My job for the past four summers has been as a counselor at a day camp for elementary school children. One afternoon while the campers were doing an art project, we counselors smelled something vulgar. We subtly sniffed each camper until

I realized that the stench was coming from a cute little kindergartner boy. A bad smell plus a newly potty trained camper could only mean one thing and no one wanted to deal with it. Taking a leadership role, I took the boy aside to make sure that everything was alright. Not only was this a chance to take care of the camper, but it also gave me some time to get to know the boy personally, building a bridge between the both of us.

After I had discreetly pulled the boy away from the group so as to avoid embarrassment, we headed towards the boy's bathroom. Once inside, the camper confessed that he had soiled his pants during the excitement of the group games. The solution to this situation seemed clear-cut: the boy would change into clean clothes and go out to play with a smile. However, the boy had no clean clothes to change into and adamantly refused to wear any other clothes. This is where I had to get flexible. The boy could not remain in his dirty underwear, that would be cruel and ostracizing. I would not just sit outside the boy's stall keeping him company until his mother arrived either. Like a Prius, I went the extra distance. I felt compassion for the boy and wanted to do everything I could to minimize his discomfort in the present situation. So, I found myself washing out chunky brown underwear in a bathroom sink at the boy's request. In the end, the camper rejoined the group with a smile on his face, no indignity suffered, and I learned something about myself. I learned there is great freedom in forgetting myself and being fully present with another human being. I was there for that camper in his time of need and the connection between us still exists years later. When one person in a society suffers, the whole community feels the negative energy. By taking care of the camper, he did not suffer and the connection I made strengthened the camp community as a whole, Prius style.

I have many talents. I am a gifted student, I love music, and I enjoy sports. The most important quality I will bring to campus life is the ability to connect people and myself using my sense of compassion and leadership skills, forming harmony out of diversity. My ability to lead and compassion for others are not just words. They make things happen in life. They are the traits that my peers respect as they have elected me Secretary, Vice President, and currently President of my 120 member nationally known Temple Youth Group. Being part of a strong community is important to me; I thrive in diversity as I can always find something to connect to, something to learn. I strive to maintain a strong community and to meet the needs of those members, even if they are the needs of a kindergartener.

ANALYSIS

"The Prius of My Class" makes use of an original controlling metaphor. The first line inspires the reader's curiosity—what exactly does it mean to be "the Prius of my class"? The author quickly resolves the mystery in the next lines, clearly elucidating the essay's main arguments. He introduces key words and phrases—"compassion and leadership" and "go the distance"—that become touchstones throughout the essay. In a short essay, especially, overusing the same phrases is a common mistake. In this case, though, the author uses repetition to tie his essay together. He doesn't repeat key phrases so much that they become tiresome. Instead, he uses them as unifying elements that link the essay's content to its overriding message as presented in the introductory paragraph. He also uses repetition to humorous effect, as in the recurrence of the phrase "fully loaded" to describe a Prius packed with features and a kindergartener packed with, well, something else. Sophisticated uses of language like these make it obvious that the author crafted his essay very carefully.

The scene that the essay presents in the second paragraph is skillfully evoked. When the author asks us to "imagine being outside on a gorgeous day," readers get ready to roll our eyes at a tired description of a lovely afternoon. The author makes use of that expectation to amplify the element of surprise when he reveals the unpleasant event at the center of the essay. It's a clever move, because it shows that the author is sly enough to employ a cliché yet mock it at the same time.

In some ways, the incident at the heart of the piece is a fairly mundane one. It certainly doesn't scream, "Write a college essay about me!" But it's memorable and it fulfills the most important function of a college essay: providing a meaningful glimpse into the author's mind. The third paragraph walks the reader through his thought process, showing that his claim of being a compassionate leader is borne out by his thoughts and actions. For instance, few people would see a kindergartener's potty training pitfall as an opportunity "to get to know the boy personally, building a bridge between the both of us." Besides the insights it facilitates, the story is just plain memorable, especially when combined with the inventive Prius metaphor.

The only weakness of the essay worth mentioning is that its final paragraph strays a bit too close to reiterating a laundry list of accomplishments from the author's resume. The paragraph is redeemed by the tie-in to the kindergarten story in the final line.

"Ninth Grade Robotics"

Alex Richard

THOUGH YOU WOULDN'T GUESS IT TODAY, I once dismissed math
and science and preferred to spend my time reading history books. My
interests began to expand my freshman year, but what truly solidified
the shift in my goals was my sink-or-swim attempt later that year to
teach myself to create a Computer-Aided Design (CAD)—while simultaneously producing one for my Robotics team and participating in a
national CAD contest. A CAD is used to plan out schematic designs
(in this case for a robot) which offer great detail, specifying where each
component will go and how they will be connected before construction
begins. Though my efforts didn't succeed, they taught me a great deal
about CADing and myself: they showcased my determination, self-motivation, and initiative.

Every year, nearly 10% of the students at my school shut down their
extracurricular lives, to participate in the FIRST Robotics Competition.
In six weeks we build and program a robot, and produce an animation,
CAD, and website. Although I later became Team Captain, nothing I've
done since has had as great an impact on me as that first year, when I
was the team's CAD leader; it inspired all of my later participation on
the team.

Every night for six weeks, after the main robotics meeting finished,
I would spend hours laboriously transferring the day's progress into
the program used, Autodesk Inventor. I'd never CADed before, and
only downloaded Inventor the night we began; that was the day after
the Design Captain resigned, leaving me as the only team member. (I
also had no experience with the actual construction, so I didn't know
enough to produce any realistic designs.) Naturally, I fell badly behind
the actual production in the first weeks. But even though nobody really expected me to successfully produce a design and I knew that the
design would be useless, I carried on. In general, I tend not to relent
once I've started something, since I feel socially committed to doing it
and I (irrationally) don't want to lose sunk costs.

As the weeks passed, I did learn, and made genuine progress on the
design. I still remember how excited I was when, after hours of staring, squint-eyed, at the laptop in the darkness, as power metal and rap

blared in my headphones, I zoomed out from the individual connections between parts to see the first draft of the entire design.

My design didn't place, of course; it wasn't particularly competently made. The actual value of the design was in the lessons it taught me: not merely the knowledge of CAD, but also, more importantly, the work ethic—that if something needs to be done, then you find a way to do it, no matter how ill-prepared you are. The next year, my design was selected out of hundreds of other designs to be a National Semi-Finalist. And today, the design team members—triple in size—enthusiastically await this year's challenge, which we will tackle in cooperation with the overall robotics team.

ANALYSIS

The structure of "Ninth Grade Robotics" is easily visible to even the most casual reader. From the start of the essay, Alex indicates that he will show how his attempt at using CAD, though a seeming failure, actually taught him important skills and "showcased [his] determination, self-motivation, and initiative." He goes on to illustrate this point with some storytelling, always tying his points back to his main idea at key moments. For instance, he goes back to the touchstone of his thesis in the lines, "In general, I tend not to relent once I've started something, since I feel socially committed to doing it and I (irrationally) don't want to lose sunk costs," and "The actual value of the design was in the lessons it taught me." Even within the limited space of a college essay, it never hurts to hearken back to your main idea as you develop your argument or storyline. Markers like this help remind the reader why you've made the choices about what to discuss in the body of your essay and ensure that they will have a firm grasp of your take-away message. In the conclusion of his work, Alex provides a small surprise for the reader by noting his subsequent CAD success. Since the essay is centered on failure, this revelation makes more of an impact on readers than it might have otherwise. After all, we've spent the bulk of the essay rooting for the underdog, so we're especially inclined to celebrate his ultimate success.

Telling details add flavor to the raw ingredients of the piece's argumentative structure. Alex gives the backstory of how he found himself left with all the CAD responsibilities, which makes his plight more dramatic. He brings readers into the darkened room with him when, "after hours of staring, squint-eyed, at the laptop in the darkness, as power metal and rap blared in [his] headphones," he experiences a breakthrough in understanding CAD. The details help heighten the interest of a moment that could otherwise seem insignificant. Imagine how much duller the line would be if Alex had instead written, "One night I had an epiphany about how the design was coming together in CAD." Learning some sensory details helps readers picture the scene and empathize with Alex. In addition, finding out what kind of music Alex listens to while he works makes readers feel they are getting to know him on a personal level.

The moment of epiphany also illustrates the essay's evocation of both the internal and external stakes of Alex's project. Alex can step back and reflect on what internal elements in his own character made him determined to learn CAD, while also recognizing his external responsibilities to his teammates. Almost any college essay will tell the story of an epiphany you had and/or a situation where you felt something significant was at stake. Try considering what details you can add to make your epiphany feel more immediate to the reader, as Alex does so successfully. Also think about ways to convey the personal and relational aspects of a dilemma or a challenge. Often, both your pride and others' expectations come into play, and it could be interesting to develop one or both of these angles in your essay.

"Treaty of Versailles"

Jackie Botts

Essay prompt: An intellectually engaging idea or experience

BY THE SECOND DAY OF OUR mock Treaty of Versailles, the class had been reduced to a shouting match. The German contingency bellowed that Russian mobilization had amplified the Balkan conflict into a global war, while the Austrian representatives shouted that the assassination of Archduke Franz Ferdinand had forced them into war. Meanwhile, USA and France were fiercely debating the moral obligations of victors.

Up until now, the other moderator and I had facilitated the discussion smoothly. Besides an occasional flare-up over the fate of Alsace-Lorraine or German disarmament, a more fair and just peace was beginning to take shape. As moderators, our task was to hammer out a lasting peace. In preparation, we had pored over textbooks and timelines, charts, historical analyses, and primary documents for three days. We had charted each nation's agenda, war actions, and potential concessions. With the hindsight of history, we had attempted to look at the facts objectively and rationally. It was finally time to hear the nations speak.

I'd been elected to moderate because I'm a questioner and a listener by nature. I like to consider each side and I am notorious among my friends for my pros and cons lists. Thus I was in my element, able to direct conversation, offer ideas, and propose questions. In front of a classroom of 30 passionate diplomats and a mess of charts, maps, and text books, we finally worked out a treaty that was unanimously accepted. It involved a less vindictive reparations plan, territorial settlements that denied imperialistic impulses, and a disarmament program designed not to punish Germany but to reduce European militarism.

For several days, I was utterly immersed in the European dilemma of 1919. After I had carefully sifted through the facts and opinions, tapped into the collective intellect of historians, listened to my peers, and weighed each option, I finally arrived at a conclusion: a kick-ass Treaty of Versailles and my own analytical process.

ANALYSIS

Jackie's "Treaty of Versailles" begins with a vivid description of a room full of diplomats fighting tooth and nail. These exciting events, told in Jackie's rich narrative style, engage her audience. Her ability to take a simple classroom activity and bring it to life is what makes her essay stand out from a pile. However, Jackie ultimately succeeds because she is able to use this singular event in order to illustrate her own intellectual vitality. For example, by referring to her peers as "the German contingency" and "Austrian representatives" Jackie implies that she is able to grapple with issues that reside in a global context. Likewise, her ultimate ability to pacify her peers who are "debating the moral obligations of victors," proves that Jackie can calmly and actively think through deep, philosophical issues.

The second paragraph, maintains the narrative tone. Jackie keeps up the charade that it is up to her class to determine "the fate of Alsace-Lorraine or German disarmament." This effect provides both continuity and color for the essay. Moreover, Jackie slowly begins to elaborate on what she was specifically able to contribute to the group project. Mentioning her experience with "timelines, charts, historical analyses, and primary documents," highlights both the breadth and depth of Jackie's research capabilities. Meanwhile, her acknowledgement that she had the "hindsight of history" on her side shows both modesty and an awareness of her circumstances.

By the middle of the essay Jackie stops alluding to her characteristic strengths and instead starts explicitly explaining why she was chosen to be moderator. This is a risky move, especially when considering how effectively she applied the "show don't tell" rule in the first half of her essay. Still, her strategy works well because she frames this bluntness with sincere observations. When she describes herself as "a questioner and a listener by nature," she also notes that this is how others see her— she is "notorious among [her] friends for [her] pros and cons lists." Providing this context allows readers to therefore interpret her self-description as an honest reflection, instead of bragging. Additionally, the use of the second person plural ("we finally worked out a treaty" instead of "I finally worked out a treaty") shows that Jackie was willing to give due credit to the success of an entire team, and not just herself. This humility overshadows the frankness in the beginning of the paragraph.

Jackie's last paragraph could be strengthened in terms of content. She simply re-states information that appeared earlier in the essay. The conclusion would have been more effective if she talked about what exactly she learned or how she grew from this particular experience. Still, the voice in her final line about the "kick-ass" fruits of her labor, sound like the real words of a high school student, moreso then the rest of her essay. In the end, we get the sense that Jackie is a student who is as enthusiastic about academic challenges as she is capable of undertaking them.

14

PERSONAL GROWTH

"Silence"

Marisa G. Messina

SILENCE. IT'S A LOUD WORD, EVEN for a talkative person like me. It gets my attention, startles my other senses awake when my ears have nothing to process. Often, silence feels uncomfortable to me. But I'm learning that sometimes, foreign as it is, silence is not a bad thing.

Reticence is not often in my routine. I love to think, and talking helps me crystallize my thoughts, so I'm generally rather verbal. I always considered my articulateness just a manifestation of confidence: I'm bold enough to share my ideas.

But one phrase, a pearl dropped by the leadership facilitator at a summer conference, changed my approach. "You don't learn anything when you're talking." It was shockingly acute, and burned right through my old beliefs about silence. How one-sided I'd been in thinking that my filling of "awkward" pauses was generous, contributory! On the contrary, I'd been unintentionally squelching the opportunity for others to reflect unhurriedly and to respond of their own accord.

So, I accepted the leadership guru's personal challenge for me: to remain completely silent for an hour.

It sounded simple but proved strenuous. I tried to use gestures and actions to express myself, but communicating without words was much harder than I expected it to be. I failed my first two attempts after less than twenty minutes. The first time, we were at the zoo, and the label for the Styrofoam giraffe hat at the gift store was printed only in French. Excitedly, I tried to translate it for my friends—from French to charades. I became so animated in explaining Cleo the Giraffe's habitat and eating habits that I let escape the word "between" without even realizing it. Shoot. The second time, a man held the door for me out of the gift shop and I said, "Thank you." The third time, my determination quietly revved into high gear. In silence, I navigated the Metro, purchased a birthday gift, and ate a meal at Potbelly in the company of my loquacious friends. I was a fly eavesdropping on their conversation, my head buzzing with unexpressed thoughts but simultaneously free from the need to engage.

At first, I couldn't let go of my desire to speak. My friends' conversation lent itself perfectly to my anecdotes, but I couldn't contribute them. It was maddening listening to their banter and hearing the caged voice in my head, loud but futile. I tried writing myself draft text messages of things I wanted to mention when the hour was over, but I could barely keep up as the conversation wandered.

So then, I began to let go. I just drifted through the conversation, listening, observing, enjoying. I noted the pauses in conversation, the silent parts during which I would normally have spoken up. Instead, someone else filled the void—and said something more profound than I probably would have. And I understood.

There's a scary aspect to remaining silent: I didn't know what other people would say, and, without being able to respond, I had to rely on their ideas and opinions to govern the conversation. What if they started talking about something I knew nothing about? Or, what if I could have added something to the discussion that would have deepened it for my fellow interlocutors?

What if I hadn't spoken up that time on the cross-country team bus as we departed, asking "Where's Patrick?" He might still be at the Brandywine Creek State Park cross-country course, waiting for a ride… What if I hadn't pulled Carter aside on that first day of Spanish camp when I saw tears on her face? Would someone else have checked in with her, offered her a hug and a dose of empathy? My conversation with her allowed her to talk; instead of expending the collective quota for talking, I was expanding it, providing space for conversation.

So is being silent being greedy, because it allows me to separate myself from the turmoil in everyone else's lives, and it allows me to soak in others' ideas without contributing any of my own? But, on the other extreme, talking too much can squelch others' space to ponder. So where's the balance? When to talk, when not to talk?

Shhh, I'm still thinking. Silence, please.

ANALYSIS

Marisa's essay on silence is a testament to her personal growth. There are times when the essay focuses on Marisa's negative attributes; for example, she admits that she talks more than she listens. However, Marisa is able to humbly take a step back, and look objectively at her experiences. Over the course of her story about learning to value silence, Marisa becomes a more mature and thoughtful person.

The essay begins with a bit of a rough start. Marisa's language is heavy with five dollar words that often don't add much to the content of her essay. Furthermore, sentences like "I always considered my articulateness just a manifestation of confidence," are awkwardly worded. As a result, Marisa seems to be trying too hard to impress her reader. If Marisa had opened the essay using simpler, more straightforward language, she could have been easier to understand.

However, Marisa's language use changes over the course of the essay, marking both her maturity as a writer, and as a person. The essay picks up in the fourth paragraph, when Marisa accepts the challenge to not speak for an hour. Her anecdote about trying to translate French into charades is funny, and endearing. Ironically, in her silence, Marisa becomes more in tune with her personal voice. Sentences like, "I let escape the word 'between' without even realizing it. Shoot," sound more honest, and are more engaging than phrases from the beginning of her essay. This increasingly sincere tone continues throughout Marisa's narration of her failure to stay silent.

At first Marisa's silence allows her to understand the importance of hearing other people's opinions. This would have been an appropriate place to end the essay. If Marisa had stopped writing here, she would have gone through a full character arc. She was a talkative girl, who learned the value of stepping back and listening to those around her.

This is a typical structure of a college essay; a student talks about how they had a particular experience and then walked away having learned a valuable lesson. Instead of following this pattern, Marisa tries to end by analyzing the actual significance of the lesson she learned. She considers how the positive attributes of silence, mainly gaining the insights of others, weigh against the positive assets to speaking out for people who are not able to speak for themselves. In a few short anecdotes, Marisa points out why silence is not always the answer. In this way, Marisa proves that she is a deep thinker, constantly considering the consequences of her actions. In the end, Marisa's ability to glean the nuances of the advice offered to her is what makes her essay so effective.

"The Artist of My Everyday"

Anonymous

MANY PEOPLE HAVE HELPED SHAPE MY personality and character in ways I do not regret, though the remnants they leave within me are sometimes bittersweet. Beyond my family, no one has affected me more than my ballet teacher of eleven years. From a young age, I emulated her. Her presence and support helped to define my work ethic in ballet and in many other realms. Even now, though I have not done ballet for over a year, the facets of her personality that I adopted are still a strong presence in mine, and my interactions with her, though rare, affect me greatly.

She is the most selfless person I know. She is the most self-effacing person I know. She is the bravest, the strongest, the saddest, the most intensely diligent. In all of these things, she is what I tried to become, be it for better or worse. She formed my outward composure and internal contradictions. Being so like her, she understood me from a young age, and I could bare myself to her as a result. By her example, I decided quite young to never be satisfied with myself; she is the only person I believed when she said, "You're worth it." Because of her, I decided to always try to hide pain; she is the only person I cried in front of after I could help it.

Above all else, she is the voice reminding me that nothing is worthwhile without diligence. In all undertakings, I hear her as she often spoke to my class: "If you're not going to put everything into what you're doing, why are you here? If you don't try, you're just wasting your time. You could be doing so many other things right now." Of all that my teacher has given me, this mentality is by far the most positive and, in terms of the quotidian details of my life, the most useful. I endeavor to apply it to every aspect of my life, starting with ballet and quickly extending to school and personal projects. As important as other elements of my personality might be in defining my perceptions and analyses of the world around me, this element largely defines my internal dynamics.

I continued in ballet longer than I perhaps should have because of my teacher's presence. Ultimately I stopped because of an injury. I talk to my teacher occasionally. Afterward, I am always inspired to work harder, be stronger, and think evermore of others over myself. She has taught me the mold for my everyday, and interacting with her again always reinforces the setting in this mold. Her influence has been so integral to who I am that it is difficult to say whether it is for better or worse. In shaping my actions it has been for the better, but in developing my sense of self-worth perhaps for the worse. Nonetheless, the qualities she instilled push me through whatever obstacles I might face. I am forever glad of her presence.

ANALYSIS

This essay looks holistically at what it means to have a role model. The author notes that many people have had an influence on her, in both positive and negative ways. She doesn't try to candy coat her essay by claiming that everything she's learned from adults has been positive. Likewise, the author is willing to admit that many people have made her the person she is today before confining herself to discussing how her ballet teacher specifically influenced her life.

The relationship between the author and her teacher is interesting. Even though an injury prevents the author from continuing dance, she maintains a relationship with her mentor. They meet occasionally, and the author relishes the opportunity to re-connect to an adult who has been influential for her. This is important to note because colleges expect students to develop strong, significant relationships with other students, professors and alumni and stay connected to these people after college. In turn, the author has proven that she is capable of developing and maintaining these types relationships.

In the second paragraph, the author starts to explain how her ballet teacher influenced her, both positively and negatively. The author never directly names which traits she picked up, but we are left to assume that the author becomes selfless, self-effacing, brave, strong, sad and diligent, just like her mentor. More details about why the author adopted these specific traits, and how they each affected her personality, would have added more depth to this paragraph. Additionally, she could have added more detail to avoid confusing contradictions. For example, the author notes that her ballet teacher taught her to never be satisfied with herself. At the same time, her dance teacher is the one who teaches the author about her self worth. This and other contradictions are never fully explained, making this paragraph a bit confusing for the reader.

The third paragraph corrects for this by effectively explaining how the lessons the author learned from her mentor affected the rest of her life. She starts by stating that her ballet teacher taught her the importance of diligence. A quote then lets the reader hear the ballet teacher convey this wisdom in her own words. Finally the author explains how this insight has affected her dance, schoolwork and personal life. The organization of this paragraph therefore allows for a substantial understanding of exactly how the author's ballet teacher acted as such a potent mentor. This form would have been effective, if it was used for the other paragraphs in the essay.

The author could have ended the essay here, as the final paragraph could have been used to develop ideas about how other traits, such as selflessness and bravery, came from her instructor. In this case, she could have chosen fewer characteristics to describe, and described each in more detail.

"Refuting Samson"

Nathan Tindall

HAIR, LIKE LIFE, IS A REMARKABLE *thing, constantly growing, yet at an unperceivable rate, until a catalyst imparts a drastic change.*

I was my hair. Thick, side-swept, chocolate colored strands cascaded down from my scalp and fell below my shoulders. It was long, but I liked it that way. As my hair grew, it became a part of me, central to my identity. My mother constantly pleaded with me to cut it, saying, "No one can see your handsome face!" I didn't care—this was who I was.

It happened in a hallway during my sophomore year. I was sitting on the floor, waiting for the morning bell to ring, playing with my hair, feeling the strands tickle my cheek. A girl, memorable and blunt, said to me, "You know, no one is going to take you seriously with your long hair." Her words shook the pillars upholding my identity: the honesty broke through my mother's coddling. I managed a meager response, but I was stricken. Did the world really have qualms about me because of the way I looked? Was my mother right? Did my appearance hide who I was?

The words echoed in my mind over the next two weeks, starting as an intermittent whisper and heightening into profound worry. I feared that I would never discover my niche without changing the core of my identity. My individuality was caught between my heart and the world. I came to believe that the world controlled who I was—that I was no more than what others perceived of me. I wanted to be accepted, to be respected, to be great. So I cut it.

It was an act of acquiescence, of unadulterated weakness. After trimming my identity, I expected a sweeping transformation to occur in my life that would suddenly bring me much closer to my dreams. I hoped that by changing my outside, I would change on the inside. Once the shock wore off, the world adjusted, and I was still the same person. Nothing changed. They may have perceived me differently, but the image I saw in a mirror was the same: original, passionate, human, myself.

I believe that society can see beyond the apparent to recognize the faded impulses of humanity, the exceptional things that define each one of us. Looking back, I realize that my identity doesn't come from what the world perceives of me, but rather who I believe myself to be. My moment of shortsightedness did not weaken me; on the contrary, it strengthened me. Trimming my identity to fit into what I thought the world wanted me to be made me appreciate the importance of keeping myself whole. I am not Samson: my hair isn't everything to me. It isn't what makes me distinctive; it isn't how I'm going to change the world. The source of my ability is my belief in self, the confidence to be unique, the willingness to throw down my inhibitions and *live*!

ANALYSIS

Nathan's essay explores his sense of identity by examining his outward appearance, particularly his hair. Coming through most strongly in this essay are Nathan's passionate personality and his penchant for philosophical reflection. The writing style is individualized. On one hand, some of the descriptions and ideas may seem overly dramatized (such as when Nathan describes his hair; "Thick, side-swept, chocolate colored strands cascaded down from my scalp…") yet the writing portrays the student's uniqueness and illustrates that he's comfortable in his own skin.

Choosing the topic of hair for a college essay may at first seem an out of the ordinary choice, but Nathan is able to take his chosen topic and use it to delve more deeply into his held beliefs and opinions. Nathan has long hair that he admires and that he believes represents a central part of his identity, however comments from his mother and a classmate about how his long hair may cause others to perceive him negatively, makes Nathan doubt whether his long hair represents him. Nathan cuts his hair. The act of cutting his hair reveals to Nathan that his hair is not who he is, however, who he considers himself to be is more clear to him after he cuts his hair. Nathan says, "After trimming my identity [hair], I expected a sweeping transformation to occur in my life that would suddenly bring me much closer to my dreams. I hoped that by changing my outside, I would change on the inside." The essay progresses from consideration of outward appearance to contemplation of the inward self; Nathan begins the essay with describing his hair and transitions to contemplating his "core": "Looking back, I realize that my identity doesn't come from what the world perceives of me, but rather who I believe myself to be." The progression in Nathan's essay works seamlessly with its subject, the essay deepens in seriousness as the essay develops and his considerations of the topic of his hair move from lingering details about his hair to consideration of his internal make-up.

There are moments in the writing when the ideas are difficult to follow, the sentence "I feared that I would never discover my niche without changing the core of my identity." could use further explanation to understand why Nathan believes this to be true. Nathan also writes "I believe that society can see beyond the apparent to recognize the faded impulses of humanity…", which could use rewording so his meaning with the phrase "impulses of humanity" is less abstract and more concrete.

Nathan's essay ends emphatically, "It [his hair] isn't what makes me distinctive; it isn't how I'm going to change the world. The source of my ability is my belief in self, the confidence to be unique, the willingness to throw down my inhibitions and *live!*" The phrase "throw down my inhibitions and *live!*" feels authentic and conveys a great deal of personality. Overall, it's Nathan's personality and philosophical thoughts shining through in the writing that make for a memorable essay.

"A Friend in the Making"

Brian Tashjian

Essay prompt: A note to your future roommate

HEY ROOMMATE!

I'm Brian but a lot of my friends and teachers call me Btash. I have a pretty close family with two little sisters and my mom and dad. I'm hardly ever home these days because I'm always at school or work or out with friends. And despite my parents' attempts to keep me a child, I think I am ready to begin Freshman year. I'm really looking forward to meeting you! Are you as excited about college as I am? I figured since we will be rooming together for this first year, I should tell you a little about myself. But the truth is: I'm more excited to learn about you!

People fascinate me. I enjoy being around people and getting to know them for who they really are. I like the meeting, the conversing, the laughing, the learning. Every day I learn something new about my closest friends that I didn't know before, and everyday our relationships grow stronger. Often times when people, including some of my friends, are going through tough times, they yearn for some time alone, time away from everyone and everything. I am the opposite: I need someone to talk to, I need to get closer rather than far away, and that is why I am so excited to get to know you. Trusting people has never been difficult for me and I look forward to having conversations with you about anything and everything.

Working well with others is my most important goal, and that is not only for school work. Working on homework or projects in the same place as someone else, knowing they are studying just as hard as I am, helps me stay focused, but I can't wait to work with you and everyone else on dorm activities or anything we do as a class. I work well with nearly everyone because I come in contact with all different kinds of people at school, work, and on the tennis court. There is no doubt in my mind that we will get along as roommates, work partners, and friends. I look forward to really getting to know you, friend. I can't wait until the day we meet!

Sincerely,
Btash

ANALYSIS

It would be easy to make a "Letter to My Roommate" essay all about the author, rather than about the roommate. Brian (or should I say "Btash"?) makes the roommate the focus of his essay, demonstrating his consideration for others, while still communicating important facets of his own character. He even makes this idea explicit by writing, "But the truth is: I'm more excited to learn about you!" It quickly becomes clear that Brian thrives on engaging with those around him. He talks about his everyday interactions, his love of "the meeting, the conversing, the laughing, the learning" and also mentions that his preferred method of handling difficult times is seeking comfort from friends. Not everyone would think to talk about their personal coping strategies in an essay like this, but Brian makes it work. Describing how you react to stress can reveal a lot about who you are. What's more, like everything Brian mentions in the essay, it is directly relevant to how he will interact with his roommate. That fact alone shows consideration. Brian doesn't ramble too far afield about what he's interested in and what he's done in life, but rather maintains a direct link to information a roommate would like to know. It's important to learn, for instance, that Brian likes to study with other people.

The section in which Brian discusses working with others succeeds because he gives heft to what otherwise could be a pretty meaningless statement. After all, many kindergarteners come home with "Works well with others" scrawled on their report cards. Brian makes this claim real with examples of the contexts in which he likes to collaborate—examples carefully tailored to his anticipated future at Stanford. He portrays himself not only as a good roommate, but also as a student who can make important contributions to his dorm and his class.

Brian's decision to pepper his essay with descriptions of how eager he is to meet his roommate conveys more enthusiasm than any amount of exclamation points ever could. (On that note, keep in mind that in a short essay, one use of an explanation point is probably more than enough.) He repeatedly returns to the theme of how excited he is to meet and get to know his roommate, showing that it is not just an offhand claim scribbled into one sentence and abandoned. He even engages his future roommate with a question: "Are you as excited about college as I am?" Brian capitalizes on the roommate letter prompt as an opportunity to showcase his ability to engage with others.

"Learning to Read"

Devney Hamilton

I WAS FOUR AND PUZZLING OVER shapes that made letters. My parents assured me I would learn to read soon enough, but I could not wait to unlock the stories in books by myself. Once I broke down the door to printed words, I begged my family for stories I knew I wouldn't find in books. Grandad's and Nan's stories, dinner conversations, and the chronicles of Kim, Peter Pan, and Lyra wove themselves into a nascent faith that helping strangers never hurt anyone, that hardship inevitably led to savvy and independence that made me green with envy, and that self-reliance was hope's invincible weapon.

Then I was seventeen and puzzling over shapes that made letters. I could not fathom the graffiti on a flood wall by the Mississippi River. No amount of squinting, stepping back, or cocking my head would show me the meaning. But this time, no one told me I would understand it soon enough.

I was at that flood wall because of my summer class in urban studies, which also took me to a certain stretch of Martin Luther King Boulevard in St. Louis. The outsiders usually roll up MLK armored in expensive cars. We walked. The people who seem to belong in the neighborhood tagged my classmates and me as curiosities or intruders from blocks away. Even in our ignorance of the visual guide to who's who on MLK, we had no trouble reading the clothing and stance of the woman we were approaching in the shadow of one particular boarded-up building. We were nearly past her when she asked us what we were doing on the same sidewalk she was standing on. An unsolicited thought slowed my steps: Grandad talks to everyone, and a prostitute is someone. I pushed back my usual excuses before they could quicken my step, and called my companions to come back. I caught Paul's look of wary astonishment as Liz and I stumbled through an explanation, "architecture . . . studying . . . community . . . change."

Her response washed over me in waves too big, too silt-ridden, too relentless for me to handle. Until then, I had outwitted myself, using my bittersweet arsenal of stories to build an outlook that goodness, however indefinable, balanced out the ugliness, futility, and injustice of the human condition. Now that innocence was in danger of drowning in this woman's sauntering hopelessness that was so alien to me. I could not reach out my hand to her, and that threatened to shatter my foundation of stories that proved hope a universal possibility. Later, I realized I had judged her addiction, her prostitution, and the abandonment of her children to be out of my grasp because she claimed them as her identity without self-pity and without remorse. I had been frustrated that she was not asking for change. But how could I expect her to live everyday in pity and regret?

After we walked away, we realized that someone had covertly observed our conversation and was now tailing us onto a deserted street. The next five minutes of a fear I didn't want to admit made me realize how completely out of control police must feel in the most difficult neighborhoods. It turned my blind anger at police profiling and harassment into questioning of how that could change. The incident connected individual emotion, academics, and the street into a complex material of truth for me to examine and improve. And that's when I learned how to read graffiti. The letters and perspective are contorted into an explosion of color and lines—the city in two dimensions—and the meaning is in one's reaction to it. Does it resonate? Threaten? Intrigue? Deafen? Humble? Empower?

It humbled and intrigued me, drawing me into the community's eclectic trove of stories. Six days and two blocks away from where the prostitute's story overtook me with despair, a reverend asked me when—not why or how—I would build my proposal for an arts center on MLK. No library will tell you what "endemic poverty" and "broken social fabric" mean on the ground, so I learned to read those stories in conversations with strangers and in burnt-out buildings. Their non sequiturs and contradictions merely reflect the complexities of a city's truth. In those stories are woven the resilient hope of those like the reverend, who improve their neighbors' lot with patience and energy, and the bitter hopelessness of those who succumb to spirals of neglect, violence, and segregation.

The stories on Martin Luther King Boulevard transformed for good the last vestiges of my childhood idealism. I have come to believe that helping strangers requires judicious use of resources to open doors, that hardship more often stifles rather then encourages individual potential, and that people achieve hopeful dreams through collaborations across professions and walks of life. With my old idealism and new practicality, I continue my own story in the borders I cross, the connections I build, and the ideas I render tangible.

ANALYSIS

From the first sentence, "I was four and puzzling over shapes that made letters," Devney creates and conveys a portrait of herself as a thoughtful and inquisitive individual. Indeed, by the end of the first paragraph we are able to infer that Devney was a precocious young-ster who loved to read, delves deep into literature and stories for sig-nificant truths and has a supportive extended family that values time and conversation with each other.

One of the main strengths of Devney's essay is this: through her personal narrative we learn loads about her without being told directly or getting the feeling that she's listing her interests and accomplish-ments. While she grew up in a relatively affluent and sheltered en-vironment, she's willing not only to learn about "the other side of the tracks" but also to try to empathize with peoples from other walks of life. She has broad academic interests ranging from literature to ar-chitecture to sociology but also the desire to step outside the Ivory Tower of Academia and put her learning into real-world practice. Most important, however, is that Devney *shows* us her ability to articulately self-reflect on her upbringing and her experiences and how they make her the person who is applying to a university program that, we infer, will continue to help her help others.

Using a specific incident or experience as the centerpiece of an essay is a good way to reveal and show much about yourself, however, you as the writer (as opposed to you the event participant), need to ensure that the event itself doesn't overshadow or overwhelm the self-portrait and the self-reflection that distinguishes yourself in the eyes of admissions officials. The event itself isn't really that important: the admissions readers will come across hundreds of similar stories of eye-awaking journeys, struggles to overcome adversity, etc. And you don't want your "Main Event" to appear staged: in other words, "I'm a privileged socialite who walked into the ghettos / built schools in South America / volunteered at the soup kitchen so I'd have a great topic for my college application essays." What sets Devney's essay apart is *how* she tells the story, how she reflects on her experiences and how she creates a complete and complex "story" of herself.

Use simple thematic threads to structure your reflections: using the conceit (idea) of "story" as bookends, Devney uses her relation-ship with words and language itself as the major theme throughout. Her worldview-changing trip to inner-city St. Louis and her experience talking with the prostitute and the pastor, while vivid, are but one example that supports and demonstrates Devney's own evolving relationship with words, stories, language and how she communicates with others as well as herself. If anything Devney's account suffers from lack of concrete details (a few specific words to describe the neighborhood, the woman, how and what she said, the pastor) that would convey that the experience was cradled within her soul. But as it's *her* story, she can keep the focus on her.

She starts her own story with her introduction to words, which blossom into her love of stories, tales and talking with people. Notice that while she's talking about learning words, her sophisticated and *appropriate* diction—"nascent," "savvy"—shows positive evidence of developing and internalizing her literary love and skills into expressive skills. On the flip side, towards the end of her essay her diction reveals a need to impress rather than accurately articulate: descriptives such as "eclectic trove" and "non sequiturs" better convey the completion of a SAT prep class than the multi-colored mural project of architecture, idealism, reality and community apathy and involvement she want to show that she "understands."

She recognizes that her ideals and values—self-reliance, independence and the ability to understand and empathize—stem from these stories, and that her early experiences with words and language sets up the framework with which she sees the world. This "storyline" threads its way through the rest of the essay: puzzling over graffiti begins her account of her urban studies field trip, her account of both the prostitute and pastor revolve around what each *said* and even her end-of-essay self-reflection is presented in terms of how her own story (and her idea of story) has changed and will continue in a more enlightened vein. Rather clever, Devney implies that a great university which integrates academics and social activism will be the focus of the "next chapter" and invites Stanford to audition for the role of a positive, catalytic character in "The Story of Devney." With that opportunity, what university could refuse?

"Silent But Deadly"

Nhi Yen Nguyen

ALL AREAS OF LIFE ARE INTERWOVEN and connected in unimaginable ways. Luckily, I have the uncanny ability to decipher those links. Thus, my defining quality, my capacity to instantly conjure witty associations between various topics, allows me to describe the many facets of my personality.

Interestingly, the phrase "silent but deadly" applies to me in a variety of ways. Cow flatulence—primarily composed of methane—augmented by the ill treatment of livestock on factory farms widely contributes to global warming. Environmental issues of exploitation and neglect motivate me to actively promote change by modifying personal habits, bringing attention to the problem through school club activities, and calling my community to participate in conservation efforts through advocacy in Girl Scouts of U.S.A.

Furthermore, I am habitually silent due to my intrinsic reticent nature. Though I do voice my opinions and thoughts in class when appropriate, I primarily remain quiet as I listen to discussions of teachers and peers, analyzing each statement, assessing the validity, and adding the depth of insight to my fermenting knowledge. Even when my presence verges on invisibility, the covert workings of my mind resonate with the critical and cognizant nature of the narrator of Ralph Ellison's *Invisible Man*.

In regards to deadly, I cannot be wholly compared to the enthused abolitionist John Brown who hacked his proslavery victims to pieces, but I do have a passion for justice issues, which perpetuates my commitment to community service. Because I believe that every person deserves the means to live a fulfilling life, I try to fulfill my duty to embrace compassion and work for the common good by serving the needy and breaking down barriers that separate universal manhood. I have taught underprivileged children. I have served food and organized clothing for impoverished families. I have eaten and conversed with elders, addicts, gang members, and the mentally ill. With each interaction, I grow in understanding, becoming aware of the rigid construction of society, value of relationships, and necessity to be the change I desire to see in the world.

Visual and olfactory responses that correspond to pheromones (such as flatulence) are regulated by the cerebrum, which also coordinates levels of higher thinking. Like Virginia Woolf, a brilliant writer who drowned herself because she could not cope with the hindrance of a mental disability, I strive to reach my full potential through productive use of all opportunities. Therefore, if you do not accept me into your institution, you would be limiting a great mind, inducing my death.

ANALYSIS

Content aside, the style of this essay reveals several important things about its author. First and foremost, she's a risk-taker. Not many high school students would have the sheer moxie to borrow the premise of a college essay from a joke about cow farts. Humor is one of the absolute toughest effects to pull off in writing, let alone within the constrained format of the college essay. If you think you can write a funny essay, by all means give it a try, but be sure to ask for opinions from lots of different readers—friends, teachers, relatives—as you revise. You need to make sure that what sounds good in your mind translates well to a variety of audiences. Remember, you can't predict what sort of sense of humor (if any) the admissions officer who reads your essay might have. Finally, her style tells readers that Nhi can make connections between many different fields, marshaling examples from history, literature, environmental studies and the science of olfaction.

When it comes to content, Nhi uses "silent but deadly" as an umbrella to pull together a discussion of many different aspects of her personality. Her first paragraph introduces the multiplicity of topics she'll cover and the tone she will set. You might even say that the opening lines are confusing in a positive way. They introduce a tongue-in-cheek tone that the reader can't yet pin down and signal that the essay will cover many seemingly disparate topics. At the very outset, it's unclear whether Nhi will be able to make the piece work—and then she does so in a stunningly memorable way. She packs an astounding amount of information about her life and pursuits into this essay. For instance, without launching into an exaggerated account of her life-sustaining, childhood-saving, adventure-producing, exclamation-mark-necessitating, capital-lettered Love for Literature! she shows that she is an engaged reader who can connect Virginia Woolf and Ralph Ellison to her own life. In addition, she humbly describes the range and sincerity of her community service efforts in lines like, "I have eaten and conversed with elders, addicts, gang members, and the mentally ill. With each interaction, I grow in understanding, becoming aware of the rigid construction of society, value of relationships, and necessity to be the change I desire to see in the world."

The standard advice for college essays is to stick to a relatively simple theme or argument and to provide clear guidance for the reader about where you're going. It may seem like Nhi throws that advice out the window, but her repeated use of the "silent but deadly" idea gives the essay just enough of a controlling thread to make it work. Nhi's choice to take a calculated risk makes her seem like the kind of person who will push herself at college. Unlike cow flatulence, "Silent

But Deadly" was surely a breath of fresh air to admissions officers faced with a stack of unoriginal essays.

"Narwhals and Identity"

Shabnum Sukhi Gulati

THE WELLSPRING OF LEGENDS, A MEAT that is rich in vitamin-C, a source of precious ivory, inspiration for a viral song, no two people would describe *the monodon monoceros* the same way. Thanks to effective studies in marine biology, a scientist could probably tell you the basic feeding patterns, life span, and gestation period of the narwhal. Yet, because the creature means so many different things to so many different people, it has become a social phenomenon representative of centuries of mystery. The narwhal is an enigma.

Equally as complex an animal is the teenage girl. One girl finds open books as intriguing as closed ones, evidenced by the marked up copies of everything from Charles Mills' *The Racial Contract* to Jared Diamond's *Guns, Germs and Steel* strewn across her room. The girl furiously scribbles down notes on a book that she was never assigned to read. Nobody will look at her notes, but they have to be perfect nonetheless. She just likes having them; she likes to learn.

This quiet passion for knowledge lies in stark contrast to the fierce competitor who is eager to make her knowledge actionable. She weaves her intensive research into every speech of her debate career in a tone unfailingly laden with fiery determination. Her motivation is borne from some intrinsic and insatiable thirst for a forever elusive goal. In the heat of competition, she can turn off her emotions with the flick of a switch.

A softer mind does not understand the construction of "winning" as an endpoint. So she pours herself into giving back. The girl leans down close to 62 year-old Mary's ear and guides Mary through using a computer to speak to her children. The delight dancing in the girl's eyes makes it clear that she is learning as much as she is teaching.

Another quirky girl dances with delight in her room as she dumps glitter in her hair for no apparent reason. She leaves the house in attire more fit for a Hollywood stage than a walk downtown. Unafraid to be different, she and her friends revel in the confused stares they command. She returns home tired and singing off-tone but, before she sleeps, she just has to take the quiz on pop-star Ke$ha's website and find out what her spirit animal is.

A book-worm, a debater, a perfectionist, a teacher, simply bizarre: I am all of these girls at once. So maybe it should not surprise me that no two people would describe Sukhi Gulati the same way. Thanks to effective studies in psychology, some might say that I am a textbook example of Erikson's adolescent condition "identity vs. role confusion". A historian may assert that Confucius would be frustrated at my reluctance to take on a single societal role. In fact, my mom calls me "silly putty" because, though my colors never change, I am constantly adapting. Truth be told, I have realized that I am just always going to be a little bit of a mystery or enigma. After all, Ke$ha says my spirit animal is a narwhal.

ANALYSIS

Sukhi uses the unconventional comparison between herself and a narwhal to pull together a description of different aspects of her personality. Any one of the identifying characteristics she succinctly evokes here could inspire an essay in and of itself, but together they present a fuller picture of who she is. In the hands of a less able writer, this essay could easily have been a hodgepodge of elements united only by a dull thesis like, "I am a complex person." Thankfully, though, the delightful narwhal analogy saves the day. It also reveals Sukhi's lighthearted side by allowing her to reveal that she got the idea for her college essay from the unlikeliest of places: Ke$ha's website.

The narwhal comparison is well-crafted at a more subtle level as well. Sukhi provides four distinct descriptions of the narwhal ("the wellspring of legends, a meat that is rich in vitamin-C, a source of precious ivory, inspiration for a viral song") and then creates a parallel with the five distinct versions of herself ("a book-worm, a debater, a perfectionist, a teacher, simply bizarre"). You may notice that she outlines these two sets of four characteristics in sentences with parallel structure at the beginning of her first and last paragraphs. In your own writing, look for opportunities to use parallelism to create a sense of continuity. Also, do your best to avoid near-parallels that have an unsettling effect on the reader. The effect may be subtle, but imagine the off-kilter feeling a reader might get from an essay that described four characteristics of the writer and only two characteristics of the narwhal.

Of course, none of this would matter much if the content of the essay were not already strong. One of the underlying messages of the essay is that Sukhi is a "mystery or enigma" with varied interests, and the eclectic yet unified examples in the essay are in sync with this theme. Sukhi chooses to give concrete examples at every step of the way. She explains exactly which books she has recently marked up, elaborates on her debate style, brings to life one of the people she has helped through her community service efforts and provides the reader with the memorable image of her glitter-adorned hair. She even provides well-chosen references—Erikson, Confucius, her mom—to illustrate different points of view about who she is. The essay sparkles because of its vivid specificity (and not just because of the glitter reference).

15

TALENT

"My Bakery"

Christine Tataru

FROM THE TIME I WAS OLD enough to use my Easy-Bake Oven, the art of baking has fascinated me. My mother would return home to find a formless disgusting compound on the counter and me, smiling proudly beside it, eagerly urging her to "Try some, mommy."

As my skills improved, and friends and family joyously devoured my latest experiments, I grew ambitious. The summer of my sophomore year, I decided that I wanted to let my passion grow, to see if I could *do* something with it.

Day after day, my eyes drooped with the effort of staying awake. Cookbooks littered my bedroom, obscuring the floor. No grocery store magazine was safe from my prying eye as I eagerly memorized recipes for creamy raspberry cheesecake smothered in warm ganache and blueberry muffins topped with cinnamon crumble. My notebooks filled with elaborate experiments as I contemplated absurd potential improvements to my recipes.

A few short weeks into my endeavor, I was already referring to the secretaries at the Alameda County Office by first name, so often was I on the phone with them working through the complex process of registering myself as a "business." Not until I had successfully studied for and passed a written exam to obtain my food safety manager license, filed for a catering license with the Environmental Health Department, registered for a business name, and painstakingly obtained an insurance policy could I begin to apply to individual farmers markets. Finally, a phone call from the kindly manager of the humble Fremont Market sent me squealing about the house in joy; I was to start selling my creations the following week.

After four hours in the rented commercial kitchen, Kitchen by the Hour, my idealistic, visionary expectations were shattering. The kitchen, with its high temperature industrial ovens and immense flame stoves, was betraying me. The pie crusts were crumbling in my hands, the muffins were overdone and unfrosted, the cheesecake was still completely hypothetical, and I was out of time! Frustrated, desperate, and convinced of my own inadequacy, still I refused to relinquish my dream. Discovering new energy, I vowed to myself, "I will make it to the farmer's market today if all I have to sell are broken soggy pie crusts!"

I did make it to the farmer's market. With soggy pies *and* burnt muffins.

Initially, I deemed the day a failure. My products were of lower quality than I was capable, and I had destroyed my first chance at success. However, I soon came to view this day as my biggest accomplishment. Apart from my studies, I have never worked as obsessively as I did to prepare for my bakery endeavor, and the increasing number of returning customers every week reflected my success. I learned so much about how *not* to create the perfect muffin, and about how not to open a business that I unlocked the secret to perfection. Try, again and again and again.

And so my own little fire was kindled, glowing brightly like the tiny light bulb in my old Easy-Bake Oven.

ANALYSIS

Christine starts off with an anecdote that's endearing and easy to identify with—what child hasn't had her mishaps with an Easy Bake Oven? Yet the essay quickly moves into territory that sets Christine apart as an unusual applicant. While maintaining a humorous tone that keeps things light and shows her modesty, the author reveals herself to be a young woman of remarkable determination and initiative. While many kids may have played around with an Easy Bake Oven, few teens have started their own successful baking businesses.

Christine includes some tasty details to keep the essay lively, from the specifics of the sweets she made to the vivid image of her bedroom overflowing with cookbooks to the fact that she was on a first-name basis with the secretaries at her County Office. The long list of hoops she had to jump through to make her business a reality shows her willingness to go about the process correctly and her ability to confront obstacles. She maintains a sense of humor about her own frustrations, especially in lines like, "the cheesecake was still completely hypothetical" and "I did make it to the farmer's market. With soggy pies *and* burnt muffins." She goes against expectations (and clichés) by writing that she learned "about how *not* to create the perfect muffin, and about how *not* to open a business." Quips like these keep the essay down-to-earth and relatable.

This essay could easily have been a dry list of the accomplishments of a young entrepreneur. Instead, Christine allowed her own voice and humor to come through clearly, making the essay into a delicious confection. When writing college essays, make sure they sound like *you*. Had Christine tried to play to what she thought readers wanted to hear—the success story of a capable young woman—she might have avoided mentioning the rough patches in her road to baking success. Playing up her early mishaps humanizes Christine and shows that she doesn't give up easily. The lighthearted tone of this essay makes it one of the best examples of how voice, as much as content, can help a college essay win over the audience. The essay gives a strong sense of Christine's likable personality and shows that, despite her extraordinary achievements, she doesn't take herself too seriously. The essay steers clear of grand conclusions or moralizing statements about the meaning of success, and doesn't go to great lengths to explain how Christine's baking experience will make her a successful student. All that would be overkill; the engaging story at the heart of the piece is delicious enough to serve without frosting.

"Note to My Roommate"

Ellora Karmarkar

Essay prompt: A note to your future roommate

HI, HOW ARE YOU? MY NAME is Ellora, and I'm really glad we'll be spending the next year together. Do you like to cook? I'd love to cook dinner for us sometime. Thanks to my crazy family, I finally learned how to cook. I've come a long way, considering that when I was eight, I refused to use the toaster because I thought it was far too complicated. My sister tried to force me to cook, with dismal results: burnt scrambled eggs with shell fragments and a side of black hair. I was ultimately banished from the kitchen with the exception of dishwashing detail. The insults flooded in. "You can do calculus, but you couldn't cook a tater tot to save your life!"

Fortunately, my family's snide remarks triggered my famous stubborn streak. I scrambled around in bookstores to find some version of "Indian Cuisine for Dummies." As I flipped through the books, images of buttery chicken curries floated through my head. My food-oriented upbringing kicked in and my mouth began to water. I hurried home, rolled up my sleeves, and started chopping. Under the suspicious watch of my mother, I turned out a delicious tomato chicken curry, kitchen intact. My family approved. With my persistence, I became the new chef in one day. Since I love cooking now, and dorm food gets old pretty fast, you'll probably get a taste of my curries within the week. What do you like to do for fun?

ANALYSIS

Ellora gets bonus points her for actually using a letter-like style in this essay—something that many people disregard as an artificial-sounding barrier to saying whatever it is they want to say about themselves. With Ellora, the letter format is in fact completely genuine, and this is in no small part due to her completely—it has to be said—spastic style. The frenetic, almost stream of consciousness energy with which Ellora begins and ends her letter (the completely useless, never-to-be-answered question, but believable all the same, "What do you like to do for fun?") conveys her absolute enthusiasm about meeting her new roommate and sharing with her, which instantly attracts the reader to her unpretentious and unforced compliance with the format and the genuine and heartfelt content and feeling it communicates.

But Ellora's lack of pretension and lack of inhibition in throwing herself into the letter format doesn't mean that she hasn't clearly polished it and planned out how to best use this essay to showcase her writing skill and her personal qualities. Ellora's words are striking and carefully chosen: she was "ultimately banished" from the kitchen, she "scrambled about" looking for cookbooks and finally, after her first cooking outing, leaves the "kitchen intact." And the overall structure of the essay is carefully crafted: the way that Ellora segues from her frenetic greetings to her roommate, the casual and personal anecdotes about her hijinks and failures in the kitchen, her family's mockery, to making a clear point about her own sense of determination and the positive effect her stubbornness has on her development is completely admirable. Her sense of humor and the vivid details allow Ellora to make a point about her determination and persistence that is so unstudied and so understated that it is almost assumed that Ellora can apply that to other areas of her life (calculus, for instance), but that her stubbornness will in no way hinder her from making friends with her roommate or bonding with others over more trivial matters like curry.

"My Dim Sum Summer"

Elena Musz

"JUST TASTE IT ALL! OH, AND remember that when they ask you if you want chicken fingers, they mean *actual* chicken fingers." After two weeks of exhausting work, my speech and debate coach introduced me to Dim Sum in Boston's Chinatown. I ate a diverse assortment of pork, rolls, soups, and alluringly unrecognizable appetizers with a multifarious group of extemporaneous speakers from across the globe. Back in Montana, I never had the opportunity to first-handedly experience so many cultures and international issues. In Boston, I became overfilled with new food and new ideas.

The previous spring, my speech and debate team awarded me a scholarship to fly to a nationally acclaimed extemp camp on the East Coast. At times during my past season I felt restricted by Montana's isolated geography and political homogeneity, so I was excited to study current events and rhetoric in a new landscape. I was sure it would advance my competitive goals. While I knew the experience would fill me with knowledge and strategy, I didn't realize the summer would be as rich as a serving of Dim Sum dumplings.

When I landed in Boston, I entered a new culture of thought. While scribbling down notes on daily lectures on topics ranging from macroeconomics to modern war, I became enthralled with international issues of social injustice. I found myself conversing about the morality of Arizona's immigration law at my lunch table and retiring to my dorm room with *The Economist* as my bedtime reading. The analysis of my favorite news sources was supplemented by the diverse perspectives of my professors, coaches, and friends. I began to view my articles and discussions as puzzle pieces that I fit together for my speeches' design, and I became excited to bring my new bits of understanding home.

After two weeks of demanding work and Dim Sum dinners, I felt poised to introduce my community to world conflicts. My new competitive goal was to express to my audience that extemp prompts aren't arbitrary questions asked just in order for high school students to practice their speaking skills; they are real-life dilemmas that affect our global community. Speech camp was a window of exposure to international perspectives on global issues for me, and I wanted to extend that exposure to my community. I showcased this attitude during my first tournament back in Montana, and my final speech on the significance of Aung Sun Suu Kyi's position in Myanmar both won me the championship and engaged my valley with the world beyond our mountains.

I never want to stop discussing current events and experiencing cultures that differ from my own. Competing in extemp requires a unique combination of spontaneity, intellect, and compassion that I'm determined to continuously develop throughout my life. My passions are developing in conjunction with my global awareness. Because of this, I am certain that even when my involvement in competitive speaking is complete, my mission to educate both my audience and myself will continue. Although the actual chicken fingers didn't provoke my hunger, the collaborative experience in Boston developed my appetite for intellectual and multicultural engagement.

....

ANALYSIS

This essay showcases Elena's ability to take advantage of new opportunities. Maturely, Elena notes that her home in Montana limited her intellectual growth. The homogeneity prevented her from gaining academic insights into global issues. Therefore, like a sincerely curious student, Elena found ways to overcome the constraints of her home state and seek the opportunity to better herself.

Elena shows great initiative during the entirety of her essay. First, she seeks out the opportunity to grow by agreeing to go to the extemp camp in Boston. While she was there, Elena took notes and engaged in supplementary reading outside of the camp to better herself and her understanding of the issues being discussed. Both of these actions prove how Elena took full advantage of her time, as opposed to passively sitting through lectures. Finally, Elena brings the lessons she learns home to both win a speech tournament and further educate her community. In this way, Elena was truly able to make the most of her experiences and successfully integrate them into her life outside of a two-week camp.

Furthermore, Elena's rhetorical approach to telling her story is unique, and interesting. She talks about Dim Sum in relation to the cultural knowledge she was able to consume during her time in Boston. This connection is first introduced in the opening paragraph, when Elena begins the essay by describing the food she is trying for the first time. The newness of this culinary experience correlates with the new ideas she is learning to consider. This image of experiencing new cultures through several means intuitively fits with the theme of Elena's essay. However, Elena has difficulty fully developing the metaphor. For example, in the first paragraph, Elena mentions Dim Sum and new experiences together, but she doesn't make a direct connection between the two. She doesn't go so far to say that trying Dim Sum was the same as learning about global issues. However, she does do it in the second paragraph. She notes that her summer was "rich as a serving of Dim Sum dumplings." This simile works well to connect the two running themes of her essay, trying Dim Sum and gaining exposure to new intellectual ideas. Unfortunately, Elena then drops almost all mention of Dim Sum until her final paragraph. The final sentence of the essay notes that, "Although the actual chicken fingers didn't provoke [Elena's] hunger, the collaborative experience in Boston developed [her] appetite for intellectual and multicultural engagement." The ending works well, but it would have been even more effective if Elena had developed the "intellectual Dim Sum" metaphor more, and consistently referenced it throughout the entire essay. Doing so would have made the entire essay more cohesive.

Still, Elena's essay balances the two key features of a strong college application essay. Her rhetorical style is engaging and interesting while the content of her work cogently illustrates her academic interest. Both mark the sign of a strong prospective student.

"Where I Find Myself"

Nathan Tindall

A FAN IS GENERATING WHITE NOISE in my hallway at night, preventing a melody, a memory, from entering my thoughts. I lay in my bed searching for stillness. The fan's blades are an obstacle to deliberate silence. They are an obstacle to a symphony. The whooshing rhythm lulls me to sleep.

The noise stops, I glance at my back-lit clock: it's four in the morning. Someone probably unplugged the fan—saving electricity—considering it a "waste." How easily they take away my peace of mind. It's quiet now. I roll over. I tell myself, "You can sleep, just relax." I focus on breathing: in and out. It is amazing how loud my body is at night; my heart is a bass drum and my lungs a bagpipe. I am interrupting the quiet. My protesting mind frustrates my body, which will doubtlessly be groggy in the morning. The room's violent tranquility surrounds me. Unable to relax, I imagine something unreal: a pure tone filling the room, a source of energy encompassing all emotion. It morphs and becomes an idea. I must fill this silence!

A soundless performance begins inside my head: a masterpiece, unable to be transcribed. It will never be performed again; it is a lesson on improvisation. I imagine a sound that is my reflection. The puzzle pieces of my life are laid down, forming a memory, a fragment of who I am, an arabesque. This is inspiration.

As I reflect on my existence, a somber melody begins, embracing my every thought. It is pleasant, though if another could hear it, they would probably be troubled by the unfamiliar discord. My mind is running. All that I know or have known is a part of my symphony. Debussy and Led Zeppelin, my muses, pay tribute to my musical vocabulary. My years on the piano bench dictate the tonality; my effort in the marching band reinforces my obsession with rhythm and meter; my emotional lexicon guides the expression, the passion, of the piece.

I remember accomplishment: overcoming the odds and achieving something great, even when I thought I had no chance; the trumpets sound a prideful fanfare. I remember my mistakes and regrets: the feelings of utter disappointment and betrayal; the raucous bassoons mock the trumpets, answering with equal importance, for both my deeds and my dooms make up my character. I am proud of the clamor my life has made, that I have not been still. There have been times of harmonic resolution, and times of dissonance, every one of my experiences impacting the next, changing my own perception of tomorrow. As I lay in bed, memory surging, I am the embodiment of my past. I am the absence of silence.

Feeling my body overcome my imagination, I resign. I get up from bed, walk into the hallway, and turn on the fan, reviving my only friend in the night. Tomorrow will grant me more time to make noise.

ANALYSIS

Nathan's essay "Where I Find Myself," demonstrates how simple an essay topic can be. Nathan's anecdote about sitting in bed being kept awake by the sound of music being composed in his head doesn't say anything profound about Nathan's accomplishments or experiences. It does however, effectively inform the reader of Nathan's passion for and dedication to music.

The essay starts with an eloquent image of Nathan sitting in bed. A fan on in the hallway is generating white noise, and he falls asleep. The paragraph is not long, or complex, making it easy to read. There is no indication of why the fan's white noise is so important, other than the statement that the fan's blades are the "obstacle to a symphony." This foreshadowing and lack of a thesis builds intrigue; the reader is encouraged to venture on.

In the second paragraph, Nathan's description of his room starts to include musical imagery — his heart is a "bass drum," his lungs are "bagpipes." This gradual build up is enticing and clever. Slowly but surely, Nathan shows the reader that everything in his life is music. He never has to explicitly say that he likes music. Instead, as a pure tone fills the room, and Nathan's symphony starts to play. These descriptions allow the reader to visualize something that is not physical but is incredibly interesting about Nathan, his experience of music.

The simple statement, "I must fill this silence!" encompasses the extent to which Nathan is passionate about composing. Even when home, alone in his bed, Nathan cannot escape what comes to him organically, without effort. This is reflected in his writing, which is also organic, not weighed down by SAT caliber vocab or long sentences with lots of clauses. Instead, Nathan talks more colloquially about how he is able to improvise notes and be inspired to write music about the triumphs and regrets in his life. Nathan never says that he is a good music improviser directly. Instead of trying to testify to his own aptitude for music, Nathan shows his musical knowledge by describing his creative process.

Nathan is also able to seamlessly weave in important bits of context about the rest of his musical talents. He notes that his musical inspirations range from Debussy to Led Zeppelin, therefore implying that he is knowledgeable about diverse musical styles. He also points out that he has taken piano lessons for several years and is active in a marching band. These tidbits of information fit in with the rest of the essay while giving the reader more information.

The ending of the essay is simple and logical. Nathan gets up, turns on the fan, turns off the symphony in his head and goes to bed. This ending fits well with the rest of the narrative Nathan developed.

The ending is more effective than a conclusion that tries to awkwardly squeeze in irrelevant information, such as a statement about a career goal or a "moral to the story." Although he could have, Nathan doesn't talk about how his musical passion will continue to affect his life. Instead, he subtly notes that he will continue making music indefinitely when he notes that he looks forward to making "noise" again tomorrow.

"It's All a Matter of Team"

Brian Tashjian

Essay prompt: What matters to you, and why?

ONE OF MY TEAMMATES SAID IT best on our last day of the season: "Guys, you are my family. We are all brothers." The Bellarmine tennis team is more than just a group of individual players thrown together; there is a camaraderie matched by no other group with which I have been involved. We are diverse, yet connected. We have student-athletes from all four years of high school, from different areas around the Bay, and from different family and social situations. And yet, we are all united by a shared love: "El tenis," as our Spanish teacher/coach always calls it. The tennis team matters to me because it combines two things that I love: tennis and brotherhood.

Ever since I was ten years old, the mental aspect of tennis attracted me to an otherwise physical sport. My freshman tennis coach used to always say, "Tennis is 10% physical and 90% mental." Without the mental strength to stay calm and controlled under pressure, forehands and backhands are useless. Sometimes I feel like I have two opponents in a match: me against the person on the other side of the net, and me against the person inside my head, telling me to hit a better shot.

However, despite the undeniable pressures of tennis, the brotherhood created by working together as a team helps spread the weight of the pressure over an entire group. After any given point, I am likely to hear encouraging words from my teammates on adjacent courts. Words like "Here we go Brian" or "Go Bellarmine" fly around every court, creating a two way conversation where before the only words spoken were in my head. We support each other on and off the court, and it is because we have become a family away from home, headed by a coach who relates to each one of us. I play my best tennis when my team gives me that boost of knowing that they are behind me. I know that each one of us puts everything we have into every match, whether we are playing or cheering.

....

ANALYSIS

This essay on tennis works so well because it is so simple. It would be easy to write an outline of its main ideas after just one read-through. In a college essay, that is a very good thing. You have to get across your points in a very small number of words, so your writing must show that you have clear intentions for the take-away message. That does not mean that you must know your main idea before you begin to write; different writing processes work for different people. Some students need to write their way into discovering their main ideas and then revise accordingly, while others need to ruminate on their chosen topic and then create an outline of their essay in advance. Regardless of your preferred writing methods, it is a good idea to have a friend, parent or teacher read your essay and tell you the main idea (or two— you shouldn't try to get across many more ideas than that) in their own words. If they get something different out of your essay than what you intended, go back and revise until you get your idea across as clearly as humanly possible. As painful as it may be, never forget that admissions officers can give your essay only a very quick reading. If they aren't sure what you are trying to say, your essay has not succeeded. In many cases, you will have to come to terms with the fact that you cannot do justice to a highly complex idea or topic in an essay like this.

Brian communicates two main reasons why he loves tennis: the mental challenge of the game and the brotherhood among his teammates. To describe the mental aspects of a good tennis game, he creates the clever concept of having an internal opponent "telling [him] to hit a better shot" in addition to his external opponent. It's a memorable concept that concisely communicates his attitude toward the game. He pulls off a similar feat by noting how his teammates' encouragement has a way of creating a "two way conversation where before the only words spoken were in [his] head." These kinds of phrases work well, because they force the reader to think about tennis in a new way. The metaphors are easy to remember, and their gist is clear. The sports essay is an established subgenre of the college essay, and the themes Brian uses are classics within that subgenre. He makes them fresh through clear writing and clever metaphor.

"The Other Side"

Rob Resma

Essay prompt: A note to your future roommate

DEAR FUTURE ROOMMATE,

I can't wait to meet you! It seems like a lifetime since I took my first tour in the summer before my sophomore year. Before we begin, I would like to say that although my chemical engineering choice of major with a premed program of study, it may look like I'm all math and science; however, I want to tell you about my other side. Anyways, I'll start!

First of all I take great pride in my Filipino heritage; however, although born native Filipinos, my parents decided not to teach me the language Tagalog because English was such a difficult language to learn. I know Stanford has a Tagalog program and I'm totally excited about it! You wouldn't believe how regretful it is not to know how to speak the language of your culture!

Another passion of mine is music. I could discuss classical Baroque or classical 60's rock and roll. I could rock on to Metallica or fall asleep to Yo-Yo-Ma. In addition, I materialize my love of guitar with album cover videos on YouTube and Facebook. I'm definitely going to continue to play at Stanford. The Mariachi cardinal de Stanford caught my attention. In San Antonio, Texas, the liveliness of the music produced by the mariachis always gestures me towards the fiesta!

I take an interest in art. As a child, I vacationed in Europe and saw many famous artworks in Italy, France, and London. During my senior year I took AP Art History. Although the class requires at least three hours of monotonous sketching and drawing every night, I discovered I actually took interest in learning. I joined the Art Historians Guild and now attend museum exhibits such as the Caravaggio, the Modern, and the Dallas Museum of Art.

Well we are actually short on time! I have a busy schedule this weekend starting with working at my job at Kumon, attending the Amon Carter Museum exhibit, and perfecting Asturias, one of my favorite classical guitar pieces. I bid you a happy New Year and prosperity for the rest of the year. I'll see you soon!

ANALYSIS

Rob's roommate letter is a perfect example of using an essay to round-out an application. Other aspects of your application may make you appear to fit a traditional profile—say, the student who is "all math and science"—but the essays are a chance to highlight your originality and your well-rounded interests. No one wants to come across as a boring, cookie-cutter applicant, so it might be in your interest to show a different side of yourself in your essay than what comes across in the rest of your application.

The best part of this essay is the way Rob links each of his interests to tangible things he has done or plans to do to pursue them. He is interested in his Filipino heritage, so he plans to learn Tagalog; he loves music, so he records covers to post online; he enjoys art, so he joined the Art Historians Guild. He builds up an impression of himself as an active young man willing to put in the time to act on his interests and develop his talents. It's easy for a high school student to claim an interest in art, for instance, but it's not so easy to point to accomplishments like putting in "at least three hours of monotonous sketching and drawing every night." An admissions officer reading this piece would immediately imagine Rob making the most of opportunities at Stanford. In fact, Rob even explicitly links his existing interests to activities he hopes to undertake at Stanford, like mariachi music and Tagalog classes. He also sneakily notes that he has a long-standing interest in the school by mentioning that he first visited campus in his sophomore year of high school. The essay doesn't hold back in terms of showcasing Rob's talents; keep in mind that modesty is not as highly prized in a college essay as it is in normal life. You can't be too shy about telling your reader what you can do.

The final paragraph of the letter conveys Rob's active lifestyle. After all, what you choose to do with your time says a lot about you. Describing his weekend plans is a clever device for Rob to demonstrate how his diverse interests mold his day-to-day life. Finally, although Rob could perhaps have done more in the essay to show an interest in his potential roommate, he does end on a friendly note by wishing his roommate a happy new year.

16

TRAVEL

"Learning Where I am From"

Anonymous

Essay prompt: An intellectually engaging idea or experience

THE BARTENDER'S FIRST WORDS WERE "BONSOIR, ça te dirait de boire un verre?" I mumbled something out of a phrasebook, terrified. He broke into English and offered me a coke. I paid him, and started a conversation that would last hours with the simple words, "Where are you from?"

An Oxford student studying French working as a bartender in Carcassonne, France, and born in Iran with family in America and Africa, he understandably took a while to answer the question. Within minutes, I realized he was not going to fit into my stereotype of an Iranian any more than I was going to fit into his stereotype of an ignorant American. I recognized the vast culture gap between my Western assumptions and his Middle Eastern misconceptions, but understanding his world view helped me understand my own.

As a liberal English student, he couldn't understand my hesitation to accept that the government should provide a safety net for all citizens. That night capitalism became more than an economic theory and suddenly became a force which had shaped my views in a way I had never understood before. I was a product of American capitalism and yet in realizing that I finally developed a hunger to be a truly individual thinker.

Our conversation helped me see a person cast from a different mold with a completely different set of beliefs, ideologies, and opinions without a national identity. This forced me to step outside my comfort zone and see things as a citizen of the world alongside him, not separated by countries.

When we talked about our interests, dreams, fears, and talents we seemed to share so much more than our cultures implied. Our conversation melted ideas and perspectives together. His world illuminated my own in a way that helped us both see ourselves in a new light.

ANALYSIS

"Learning Where I am From" begins with a scene: a bartender is asking for the student's order in French. The action-oriented beginning drops the reader directly into the scene and makes the reader curious to find out more about what's happening and where. The scene details a narrative anecdote about the student's recent emblematic and eye opening travel experience. A compelling beginning is necessary for engaging the reader from the first sentence, and this student decided to use an element of story to make the essay immediately grasp the reader's attention.

At the heart of this essay is the student's realization that experiencing new and different situations can lead one to a better understanding about one's own life and perspectives about the world. The student finds common ground with the waiter and gains an appreciation of the cultural differences that shape their lives. A new awareness of the cultural forces at work in the student's own life proves eye opening for him: once the student realizes how American capitalism influences and shapes his opinions, the student decides he wants to develop greater self-awareness in order to be an "individual thinker".

The student's ability to demonstrate through the retelling of an actual experience from his life that he has a curiosity for new ideas and situations helps makes this essay successful. The effect of framing his experience as a narrative lets the reader experience the moment of self-discovery and creates a memorable impression. Small but important emotional details in the writing also relay the importance of the travel experience. The speaker steps outside of his "comfort zone" in paragraph 4 and in paragraph 1 the student admits he is "terrified" during the initial conversation with the waiter when he's addressed in French and needs to reply. These hints at the student's vulnerability highlight the challenges faced in an unfamiliar situation. The speaker, amidst these feelings of fear, finds he can be open to a new experience. The student must challenge himself when speaking to the waiter to put aside the ease of stereotypes, and the student questions his own assumptions about who he is and where he is from. The essay combines emotional and intellectual analysis leading the student to see the possibilities for becoming a "citizen of the world".

Even though this essay uses story to support and enliven the student's reflections, it's important to note the student didn't overly dramatize the writing; he struck a balance between presenting a few elements of narrative and interweaving his ideas and analysis about the meaning of the narrative he has written. This essay allows the admissions committee to witness the student's approach to life, his ability to meet the challenges of new situations and the manner in which he applies thinking skills. The student acknowledges the mental roadblocks that could have kept him from participating in new experiences during his overseas trip and demonstrates that he is able to overcome fear and anxiety of the unfamiliar in order to learn something new.

17

STANFORD PROFILE QUESTIONS

AS A PART OF ITS COMMON Application Supplement, Stanford asks a series of questions to "get to know you better." Applicants are directed to write two lines or fewer. Here are examples of students' answers.

Name your favorite books, authors, films and/or musical artists.

Elements of Style, Brave New World, A Brief History of Time, Kurt Vonnegut, Ray Bradbury, U2, *Little Miss Sunshine, Aviator*

What newspapers, magazines and/or websites do you enjoy?

I read *The New York Times*, BBC, and *Le Monde* every weekend to take in different kinds of news. I like a website called The Movies Online; a place where independent filmmakers get together. I have had the chance to give directors screenplays I'm proud of and meet people from around the world.

What is the most significant challenge that society faces today?

Opportunity is not expanding at the same rate as the world is becoming globalized. Parts of the world, like the Middle East, are becoming cut off from the world economy and people without a chance to succeed are turning to radicalism.

How did you spend your last two summers?

Last summer I built a house in Mexico with my friend and his church. For the last two summers I have had the chance to travel through Europe with my uncle, from Paris to Stockholm and Corsica to London. I also worked on short films and with a London based gaming company to design and test software.

What were your favorite events (e.g., performances, exhibits, sporting events, etc.) this past year?

I have enjoyed the opportunity to not only participate, but to vote, in my first Presidential Election. My five year old niece's first dance recital reminded me to laugh no matter what's going on in life. I also enjoyed the Bastille Day celebration in Cannes, France, with my friends.

What historical moment or event do you wish you could have witnessed or participated in?

The Constitutional Congress of 1787 is a time when the greatest thinkers served the people by creating laws for the people. Not only were they capable of a solution, they created a uniquely genius and elastic solution to government that has survived hundreds of years.

What five words best describe you?

Creative: I think differently about thinking. Driven: No one ever asked me to do my homework. Grateful: I want to make good on my parents' sacrifices. Curious: I like to ask questions just to find out something I didn't know. Compassionate: If I can do something for someone, I will.

JORDAN HAARSMA

Name your favorite books, authors, films and/or musical artists.

My favorite books are *Uncle John's Bathroom Readers*. They have so much random information I'd otherwise never learn. For movies, I've always like the Bruce Willis classic, *Die Hard*. I also enjoy pointless comedy, like *Anchorman*.

What newspapers, magazines and/or websites do you enjoy?

I regularly read the *Yakima-Herald Republic* and I often get politics news from CNN.com. I just recently joined facebook.com, and I am enjoying that so far. I'm not a big fan of magazines. They have too many ads.

What is the most significant challenge that society faces today?

The restructuring of Social Security is, by far, the most significant challenge society faces today. It is such a touchy issue, but so important, reform will have to be made. The reality is if the system isn't fixed soon, my generation will not have a Social Security check to fall back on.

How did you spend your last two summers?

During my last two summers, I worked for Haarsma Hoof Care, my father's business. This past summer, I interned at the surgical department of Prosser Memorial Hospital, watching surgeries for my senior project. I also started a drive to collect cell-phones and accessories from Prosser.

What were your favorite events (e.g., performances, exhibits, sporting events, etc.) this past year?

I went to National Convention in Indianapolis to complete in Parliamentary Procedure in October. We placed second and I had a great time. The spring play put on by our school was also very good. I went to get extra credit for my English class and was pleasantly surprised. I'm not a big play person.

What qualities do you admire in people?

I look for honesty, first off. If I can't trust someone, the relationship stalls. I also look for the ability to make informed decisions. People who act rashly do not appeal to me at all. Reliability is a valuable trait, as well.

Who is your hero/from whom do you draw inspiration?

I draw inspiration from my father. He has worked hard through many undesirable circumstances to prevail, obtaining a good job, without a high school diploma. I take his work ethic and apply it to school.

How do you rejuvenate yourself?

A nice night, relaxed on the couch, watching some high quality television, is all I need to get refreshed. I rebound from a long day pretty easily, so it doesn't take much to get me going again.

What historical moment or event do you wish you could have witnessed or participated in?

If I could have witnessed a historical moment, it would have definitely been when the first man set foot on the moon. Such a memorable step for mankind would have been epic to actually see.

What five words describe you?

The five words which best describe me would be analytical, honest, opinionated, committed and diligent. I prize being a hard-worker, and if somebody asks me what I think, I'll be sure to give them an honest answer.

Jordan Haarsma is a Stanford graduate and an associate educational consultant for Cardinal Education (www.cardinaleducation.com).

18

ADVICE ON TOPICS FROM STANFORD STUDENTS

Criticizing Less

"For my Common App essay, I spent a lot of time brainstorming topics and writing drafts, and I wasted a lot of time criticizing my own essays before I was finished, as I was so afraid of portraying myself in a negative light. What in the end became my various admissions essays were all subjects I could write about passionately, without inhibition, and the idea would usually just come to me in a less than ideal public setting: for example, my 'have I convinced you essay?' was written standing up on an overcrowded bus lurching home on a snow covered, slippery freeway.

"For my Stanford essays, I chose the topics that came first to my mind, which felt the most authentic and which I could write about most fluently in my own 'voice.' I was so tired of writing admissions essays that by the time I came to the Stanford application, I started writing just to make myself happy, and I stopped being as rigidly critical of what I was putting down on paper. Somehow, that worked."

—*Inès C. Gérard-Ursin*

Thinking about Why the Topic is Important

"I start with the 'Why' first and then I move to the 'What.' I started thinking about the message I wanted to send, the lessons learned I wanted to communicate, and the values I wanted the admissions office to know I held. From there, I then crafted the essay drawing on my life experience to provide the examples that illustrate the values and lessons. The final touch is to add creativity. The Prius answer came at the very end, the final 'vehicle' used to deliver my main message. So I start with the core substance, my 'why is that important,' and work out to the 'what is my story.'"

—Anonymous

Highlighting Going Above and Beyond

"I chose to write my personal statement about a summer I spent selling baked goods at a local farmer's market. I selected baking as a topic because it is the only activity that I have ever felt truly passionate about, and because it was an area in which I could prove that I had gone 'above and beyond.' Far from being something that I had to do to impress colleges or parents, it really was something that was completely my own, and that I loved. I might add that this was the one essay that I actively enjoyed writing. By the end of the process, I had memorized every word from rewriting it so many times."

—Christine Tataru

The Importance of the Spoken Word

"I can't remember. I think I just wrote in a notebook about people and experiences that had forced me to change my priorities or relinquish my beliefs, until a sort of narrative emerged. The hard part was making it about *me* instead of about all the people I had met who were cooler than me and stories I had heard that weren't my own. I was into spoken word, so I watched a lot of spoken word on YouTube. That helped since spoken word, perhaps even more then than now, was more about telling one's own story."

—Devney Hamilton

Addressing a Topic Not Addressed Elsewhere

"For my main essay, I talked about the development of my relationship with literature and how that changed the way I looked at the world. Reading has always been important to me, and I hadn't really had a chance to fully explain its influence on me in any other place on my application."

—Jasmine H.

Balancing Modesty and Pride

"I wrote my essay on my experiences as a freshman doing CAD in robotics; I chose this topic because I knew that I wanted to write about robotics, as it is the strongest activity from the strongest part (extracurriculars) of my application. In high school, I held all sorts of leadership positions in it—team co-captain twice, plus captain at various points of the website, design, engineering, PR and finance subteams. I didn't want to come off as boasting, though—yet I also didn't want to show myself failing in any of the important roles I held later. The choice was therefore obvious—I'd massively struggled in my first year on Design team, yet was able to recover and grow stronger via these struggles."

—Alex Richard

Writing about What's Familiar

"I chose the essay topic: 'Write about a person who has a significant influence upon you.' After brainstorming for about three hours about potential ideas for all the Common App essays, nothing came to mind for all the other essay topics. I was not very informed at the time about global issues. I wasn't someone who stood out in my community. I was ordinary; however, I had pride for my ethnicity. I was proud to be a Filipino. I wrote about professional boxer, generous altruist and devoted Catholic, Manny Pacquiao."

—Rob Resma

Making a Point

"I was inspired by the topic 'Indicate a person who has had a significant influence on you, and describe that influence.' I wrote my essay about my mother's boyfriend's 7 year old son in the hopes of showing how adults and young adults can be inspired by and actually learn from the youth in today's society."

—Katherine Christel

Narrowing Down from a List

"I wrote a list trying to sum up all the things I wanted the admissions people to know about me, which included my interests, activities, passions and values. For example, my list had love of stories, passion for travel, running and the importance of being on a team, and how much my family means to me. Many of these things were already mentioned in the application, for example in the 'Activities' portion, but I wanted to be able to talk about these in my essays because I knew that just saying 'I was cross country team captain' wasn't going to cover just how much it meant to me to be a leader and an inspirational member of such a tight-knit, dedicated group—so the list included the things that mattered to me, but also WHY they mattered and why I cared.

"Then I looked at that list and tried to figure out the best way to combine these values/traits/interests into a narrative—I took a couple that were related and worked well together and basically wrote a short story. For example, in one of my essays, I used a basic overall theme of stories, because my love of stories comes from my family, makes me passionate about travel and inspired my love of History and English. I of course couldn't fit every trait into one essay, but it worked out because I had many essays to write anyway."

—*Anonymous*

Capitalizing on a Unique Background

"I am from a rural area. I grew up in Eastern Washington state and spent a lot of time working in my dad's business hooftrimming. I was also very involved in FFA, Future Farmers of America, including holding the position of chapter president and competing in two separate FFA competitions at the national level. I figured that since Stanford was a more urban and liberal school that I would be able to capitalize on my conservative and rural background to demonstrate I could bring something unique to the class.

"When I applied, I didn't know that this is pretty much exactly what you should do. I was a first-generation college student from an area where college wasn't pushed all that hard and I just thought treating my application as a sales pitch made sense."

—*Jordan Haarsma*

Selecting a Variety of Topics

"In addition to the Common Application long essay, Stanford's supplement had three other required essays. My Common Application essay was about my experience with acne during my junior year of high school. I chose this topic because it was a really difficult six months for me emotionally, and from it I learned a lot about myself and how I overcome personal challenges.

"My first Stanford supplemental essay (intellectual vitality), I wrote about an experience I had during a summer immersion trip that I took after sophomore year. I talked about how my interaction with an injured community member furthered my interest in medicine and really inspired me to seriously pursue a medical degree. I chose this topic because I felt like it said something about me, about a possible field of study for me and about how important that immersion trip was to me.

"I made my second Stanford supplemental essay (letter to my roommate) very personal. I wanted it to be something that I would actually say out loud to someone and so I simply talked about myself and what my friends call me and what I like to do and what I am excited for in college.

"My third Stanford supplemental essay (what matters to you and why) was difficult to narrow down a topic to write about. I ended up writing about my experience with my high school varsity tennis team and the bond we all shared with each other throughout our years as a team. I chose this topic because the tennis team was one of the most important commitments I had in high school and some of my best memories are with those guys."

—*Brian Tashjian*

Close Inspiration

"I chose to write about my grandmother who had just passed away. We were very close and it was an emotional time so I wanted to write about her as my inspiration."

—Kristy Wentzel

Illuminating One's Self

"I wrote about simple experiences to which people can relate. I've faced a lot of difficult obstacles in my life that are probably impossible for most to understand, but I tried to avoid writing a piece about those obstacles. Each draft said more about the circumstances of my life than about who I was. I started over. I spent time figuring out what I wanted to say about myself and then worked backwards to find experiences from my life that helped illuminate my personality."

—Anonymous

Incorporating Humor and Seriousness

"I wanted to choose something that had both humor and a deep seriousness. I also wanted something personal, something that helped shape me into who I am today. I have two gay moms, so I decided to write about the standard question, 'What does your dad do?' that always creates funny and awkward situations for me."

—Reade Levinson

Overcoming Challenges

"I selected my admissions essay topic because I knew that it had to be a significant topic that really spoke about the true essence of me. I wanted to articulate a character-defining moment that had a huge impact on me, but also explain the importance and relevance of that impact. I chose to write about personal struggles in my life and how I had overcome financial, abusive, and psychological difficulties, and how dealing with these problems made me a stronger and more mature individual. I did not write about my personal life to gain sympathy, but to show how my past did not define me, but was crucial to the shaping of the person I am today."

—Annelis Breed

Providing a Full Picture

"For my Common App essay, I wanted a topic that would allow me to discuss many of the activities I participated in and my passions. I saw myself as someone whose main strength was (and is) an ability to do a broad range of things well and wanted to highlight that. The topic that I chose, essentially answering the question 'Who are you?' (with a personal touch) provided me with the opportunity to cover that range and give, what I believe to be, a very accurate portrayal of who I was as a person and student."

—*Sammi Rose Cannold*

An Idea Just Clicking

"For my Common Application essay I chose to write about the challenges I faced when admitting that I wanted to be a writer. I chose this topic because my school counselor kept advising us to look for something that set us apart from other applicants, and since during that stage of my life I was facing the sort of challenges I described in my essay, I thought that that would be the most relevant and personal topic I could write about.

"For the Stanford Supplement on intellectual vitality, I chose to write about the meaning words have for me. I thought of this topic when I read further into the description of what the university meant by 'intellectual vitality.' They said they wanted 'to see the kind of curiosity and enthusiasm that will allow [me] to spark a lively discussion in a freshman seminar and continue the conversation at a dinner table.' That reminded me of the discussion I had had with my brother about the meaning of words, and the idea just clicked."

—*Cristina H. Mezgravis*

Being Introspective

"I wrote about my dad, in particular how my relationship changed when he almost died from a cardiac arrest. I chose the topic because I thought it showed how I have changed over the years particularly well and it served as a critical introspection, which some admissions officers like to see in their applicants."

—*Anuj Patel*

Following the Passion

"I chose to write about dance because it was the topic that I knew I could write most passionately about and would probably allow me to present myself more thoroughly then I could with any other topic. I've been dancing for most of my life and it's an important part of who I am."

—*Jackie Botts*

Something to Say

"I selected the topic: Indicate a person who has had a significant influence on you, and describe that influence. I chose this topic because it was something I hadn't written about before and that I knew I had something to say about."

—*Anonymous*

Many False Starts

"Sitting down to write my Common App essay was one of the most writers-block-inducing moments of my scholastic career. I wrote the opening paragraphs of countless essays, none of which were remotely worthy of being put onto paper. (One was about crashing my car into a pillar in a parking garage; another was about making oatmeal cookies without eggs; a third was a stream of consciousness thank-you note to my favorite teacher masquerading as essay.) Finally, after these fruitless attempts to write something captivating and illuminating and hilarious and perfect, I stepped back to think about the ultimate objective of the essay. I realized that it was my opportunity to communicate my character, to paint myself as a *person* instead of just a collection of test scores and data. I thought about the best aspects of myself—my perceptiveness, my determination, my eagerness to constantly better myself and my synergistic collaboration with others—and about the experiences I've had that exemplify those qualities. One event in particular stood out to me: the moment when I understood the power of listening as opposed to habitually speaking my mind. The resulting essay was entitled 'Silence.' It was contemplative, inquisitive, intellectual, and it emphasized the Marisa I wanted to showcase."

—Marisa G. Messina

A Favorite Memory

"I wrote about building a catapult as a Science Olympiad project. It was legitimately one of my favorite memories of high school, and it was also one of the first times I really saw textbook science coming to life."

—Jimmy Chen

A Unique Upbringing

"I wrote a descriptive piece that illustrated the Cochiti Feast Day. I chose to write about my Native American culture because I knew it demonstrated my unique upbringing on an Indian reservation. I always took what we did, our dances, and customs for granted, and never saw them as different or uncommon because other Pueblos in New Mexico had similar ceremonies. That was until I left the rez (reservation), when I started visiting schools and observing the cities and what people do, how people live. It dawned on me that I was the one living the different lifestyle, and I knew that if I could put my life-experience into words and share it, it would resonate with admissions officers."

—Red Dakota CrazyHorse

Sudden Inspiration

"My admission essay was about my relationship with my extended family. I tried many times over many days to write a 'good' essay, but never made it beyond a few forced lines. I wanted a topic that would cause me to write something honest, from the heart, so that the reader could learn something about me that couldn't be taught by transcripts. One night, I was doing something completely unrelated to essay writing when all of the sudden I knew what to write about. I took one of the pictures from our living room, went to the computer in my room and wrote the essay in under an hour. The writing isn't great, and it's not polished, but it was sincere and felt right."

—*Rolando de la Torre, Jr.*

Highlighting Various Aspects

"I went through a bunch of different topics and chose the one that had a storyline that showcased various aspects of my experiences, goals and skills."

—*Anonymous*

Sharing Lessons Learned

"For my Common App personal statement, I answered the following prompt: evaluate a significant experience, achievement, risk you have taken or ethical dilemma you have faced and its impact on you. I choose this as the topic of my essay, because I wanted to share my experience tutoring a student in foster care and the things I learned as a result."

—*Sumaya Quillian*

Writing about a Less than Positive Feeling

"The topic of my admission essay, which my mom still refers to as the 'I hate English' essay, was my struggle with English classes throughout high school. I had actually already written it for, ironically, an English class. I brainstormed some other essay topics, and even started writing some of them, but ended up selecting and editing the one I had already written. The assignment had been to write a 'personal essay,' and I couldn't resist writing about how much I disliked English class."

—*Ben L.*

19

ADVICE ON WRITING FROM STANFORD STUDENTS

One Piece of the Puzzle

"Think of the essay not as its own discrete entity but as one facet of your overall application, with all parts working together to reflect a coherent portrait of yourself. Use the essay as an opportunity to fill in any gaps that your application may have, and avoid redundancies (i.e., if your essays are basically just another reiteration of your extracurricular activities list—that's a bad sign!).

"Also keep in mind that the essay has distinct advantages over other formats like lists and transcripts and recommendations—you're able to show not just what you've accomplished, but how you *think*."

—*Jasmine H.*

Addressing Why and How

"Use college applications to really reflect on what you've learned, who you've become so far, the whys and hows of that. Then interrogate why you want to spend four years of your life in college—what do you think is there that isn't elsewhere? What if you assume college isn't the right path for you—what would you do instead? (and 'nothing' or 'fail' or 'be a bum' aren't good enough answers—if you can make real use of a college education, you could do something interesting without it, too). Explaining all that is just as important for you as for the admissions counselors. They'll spend perhaps a few minutes. You'll spend hours and days, so make it worth it for you. I still go back to my essay—because it has so much of who I am and who I want to be in it."

—*Devney Hamilton*

Tackling Multiple Drafts

"Writing multiple first drafts of your essay, with different topics, is probably worth it; it's not *that* much more effort, and you can then rely on others' feedback to select the best one to revise further.

"Don't trust Word/Writer's character count; for me, at least, the Common App website gave a different number.

"Two ideas: Write about something that seems impossible to whoever would be reading it—something that they have no idea how you would possibly achieve this. If, like me, you can't do that, then try to avoid coming off as boasting—there are very many e.g. captains of high school robotics teams applying, and nobody likes arrogant people."

—*Alex Richard*

Just Get Started

"Honestly, the hardest part about writing a college essay is getting out of the phase in which you're staring at a blank document. The trick is... *just type ideas!* Start by brainstorming all you can about the essay. Have a resume handy at the top of your document, so you can talk about whatever stands out in your profile or even better...what *isn't* reflected in your application. The essay has to *personal*. The more aspects of your personality you show, the better chances you have of appealing to the admissions officer!"

—*Rob Resma*

Taking Feedback Selectively

"Take your time. Do it as early as you can, and you will save yourself a lot of needless worry and stress, and you might also get to enjoy your vacation days. The last thing you want to go through is spending New Year's Eve on your computer checking application essays. However, if you truly are too busy to complete them before Christmas vacation rolls around, do not be too hard on yourself: just focus on writing down what is already in your head, and feel free to boast, but only a little, and only subtly. Once you are done, get your parents, your teachers, your friends, anyone, to proofread, and proofread it yourself if you must. Then, carefully select which comments you will listen to and which you will not heed at all, and be kind to all who offer to help you out."

—*Inès C. Gérard-Ursin*

Everyday Experiences are Okay

"My best piece of advice for writing a college essay would be to stop trying to find a 'traumatic experience' to separate yourself from everyone else. College admissions officers are tired of reading pity stories. You can get away with writing about an everyday experience (such as babysitting) as long as it carries a message, tells something about yourself and is done in a creative way that exhibits your writing skills. In my essay, I wrote as if the boy I was babysitting for was my boss, and I was an engineer constructing a model for the world's largest train tracks. In that way, I turned children's play into a life experience in order to give my essay about a normally boring topic a little bit of flair."

—Katherine Christel

Writing is a Process

"The best piece of advice I can give is to start early and edit often. I think I went through at least 20 different versions of this essay, and it changed drastically about ten times. And be open to criticism. Many of the ideas in here came out of talking with friends and family and if I had been close-minded and refused their help and suggestions my writing would have suffered. There is no one right thing to say, so the topic is not as important as how you explain its significance and clearly communicate your own personality. And for that you need time and many, many drafts."

—Anonymous

When to Ignore Advice

"My biggest piece of advice is: Don't worry too much about what other people say about your essays. College essays are completely different than any essay you have to write in school because there is no designated structure—no 'right' way to do it (in fact, being incredibly original and creative in your structure or topic can help you). Because there is no structure and because these essays are supposed to reflect *you*, your essays will not resemble anyone else's. And that's how it should be—you are an individual and that fact should be highlighted.

"I remember having friends read my essays, and having them tear everything to shreds, down to the very concept of the essay itself. This stressed me out a lot until I read their essays, and the only thought I had was, 'Hm. I definitely would not have done it this way.' And that's ok. I think peer editing and reviewing is a great idea, especially when it comes to grammar, concision and voice, but don't be afraid to fight or ignore certain pieces of advice if it's something you disagree with. After all, it is your essay, and when you hit submit you want to know that *your* best work is being sent out. The way I saw it, if I was to get rejected, then I wanted to get rejected because they weren't looking for me—not because someone else's voice changed what I wanted to say."

—Anonymous

Focusing on Your Uniqueness

"Market your uniqueness, but don't be cliché. Part of my job in Cardinal Education is to help students with their college essays. It's clear that elite universities are very focused on improving diversity in their class. I was fortunate to have a particularly unique background I could capitalize on but many feel like they don't. My fellow classmates, though, all had something to offer, so it's really useful to figure out what makes you tick. Why do you like the things you do? Why do you want to study what you want to study? Everyone has something that makes them weird and Stanford doesn't admit people who think they don't. They don't want to read your resume, that's what the rest of the Common App is for.

"After I was admitted to Stanford I received the acceptance letter. Handwritten on it was a note from the Vice Provost, 'Your legacy in FFA will live on.' I had marketed the most unique aspect about me, my rurality, and the letter all but acknowledged that was why I was admitted.

"As a bonus tip: Utilize your teachers. Ask for letters of recommendation early and provide your teachers with the information they need to write a good letter, whether that's your resume or specific points you'd like them to talk about. When I asked for letters, I gave my teachers my resume and asked them to play up my rural background a bit. In addition, I had two of my high school English teachers take a look at my personal statement and provide feedback. The college application process shouldn't be navigated alone."

—*Jordan Haarsma, associate educational consultant, Cardinal Education*

www.cardinaleducation.com

Getting Personal

"I think the best advice I can give to high school seniors is to write about something that really means a lot to them. College essays are meant to let colleges know who we really are and I think that writing about something that emotionally affected us either positively or negatively is the best way to let them know what is important to you. I felt like my Common Application essay was my best essay because it was the most personal. It wasn't an essay trying to tell everyone how great I was, rather it was simply a story about something that really affected me and what I learned about myself from it."

—*Brian Tashjian*

Not Thinking about What the College Wants

"I didn't really think about what the colleges wanted me to write about, but rather, I wrote about a subject of my choice. I think the less an applicant feels the need to write what they think a university wants to read, and instead writes more about what they want to write about, the better sense the university will get of that applicant. Colleges can sense when an applicant isn't true to themselves and will be less inclined to admit an individual like that."

—*Kristy Wentzel*

The Subject Doesn't Matter

"My best advice is to be confident in yourself! Don't be afraid to write about a topic that is cliché, and don't be afraid to write about one that is avant-garde. The topic of your essay does not matter at all. What does matter is how you write your essay. Other than that I strongly suggest reading your essays out loud! It really helps with editing!"

—*Nathan Tindall*

The Importance of Talking to People

"Go outside and talk to people. Talking to people can help you think about what you contribute to your family and friends and what you might contribute to your future university. It will also keep you from going crazy. Don't lock yourself in a room by yourself and stress over your applications. Relax. Reflect. And write."

—*Anonymous*

Being Self-Aware

"I think bringing self-awareness to your essay is crucial. The essay should be focused on you and reflect on how you grew into the person you are now, how whatever story or experience you are writing about has changed you, gives your essay more depth."

—*Reade Levinson*

Focusing on Significance

"The best advice for writing an admissions essay would be to really evaluate what is important to you, and to write about something that captures yourself in only 500 words. And if you decide to write about an event or activity to illustrate that, be sure to make it clear why it was significant, and how it affects/affected you on a deeper level. That distinction shows maturity and reflection."

—*Annelis Breed*

Improving over Time

"Write as many as possible. I believe that writing this type of essays is a skill that you sort of acquire over time. Looking back at my Early Action essays compared to my regular ones, I realized that the latter were a drastic improvement on the former. This can be accounted for if you write a lot from the get-go such that you're able to choose whatever best speaks to you as an applicant."

—Sammi Rose Cannold

Following Your Passion

"My best piece of advice would be to find something you really feel passionate about for an admissions essay topic. When you feel passionate about what you're writing, you really inject your personality into your words, and since your passions are unique, they make your application essay unique as well."

—Cristina H. Mezgravis

Keeping Yourself at the Forefront

"I would say that you should never leave it until the last minute. For your main essay, write it, rewrite it, rewrite it again and then rewrite it five more times. Take advantage of your English teacher and review every draft of the essay with him/her. Also, when you're writing your essay, make sure that the essay truly is about YOU. Spend less time setting up the plot of the essay and more time explaining how what you're trying to narrate pertains to you as a person."

—Anuj Patel

Choosing a Topic that Excites You

"Choose a topic that you're passionate about and could keep on writing about way past the word limit. Then do just that—write as much as you can and get it all on paper. Then when you go back and read what you've written, you'll probably be able to see pretty clearly what you should focus on—there will be a sentence or paragraph that is really compelling. I think the trick is probably identifying the topic that you can really write persuasively about."

—Jackie Botts

Being Authentic

"In writing my Common App essay and other essays particular to specific colleges, I tried to ignore the formulaic conception of college applications. The only outside resources I used were one of my teachers, to help proofread my actual writing, and my parents, to help ascertain that I was representing myself in the way I intended to and the way they knew me. I avoided engaging in conversations or looking at resources about the best ways to write application essays that will get you into college. I feel as though these methods are insincere and frequently unfair. The only advice I can give is to be authentic; nothing else is worthwhile."

—Anonymous

Starting the Day the Common App is Available

"Start early! The day the Common App went live (August 1), I printed out the prompts for every essay I needed to write (for all nine schools to which I was applying) and started to brainstorm topics. I forced myself to write an opening paragraph to accompany every essay idea I had, which helped me to hone in on which ideas were worth pursuing. By the first day of school, I had finished drafts of every essay. I handed them to my college counselors before they became inundated trying to handle everyone's essays, and I was thus able to receive really quality editing advice that improved the essays exponentially.

"This 'get it done early' approach required surrendering a portion of my sacred summer to academic affairs, but it was a very worthwhile tradeoff long-term. I had all my essays completely done by the end of November, so I was prepared to send off my applications as soon as I heard back from my EA school (Stanford); I enjoyed a delightfully relaxing winter break, while many of my peers spent their holidays painfully churning out uninspired essays."

—*Marisa G. Messina*

Not Being Lofty

"Don't be too lofty, either in your prose or in your essay topic. You're just a high schooler, and nobody expects you to have cured diseases or solved world problems. Being honest and personable goes a long way."

—*Jimmy Chen*

Your Own Story to Tell

"Be as original as you are. No one has your story or has the same life experiences. Highlight your uniqueness and tell your story in a way that is true to where you come from."

—*Red Dakota CrazyHorse*

Finding a Topic You Love

"Be honest and write about something you love. You will come out in the essay."

Rolando de la Torre, Jr.

Being Honest

"Don't make stuff up. Choose a topic that resonates with you. Use the active voice and show a positive attitude."

—*Anonymous*

Self-Reflection

"Do it yourself, about yourself and for yourself. First, don't let anyone write or over-edit your essay. The essay is your chance to tell a story and show who you are, and admissions officers can tell if your parents or college counselor wrote every other sentence.

"Second, write about something that reveals something about you. If you write about someone else, be sure the essay still speaks to who YOU are. If you write about something you've done, be sure you are writing about why you did it and how it impacted you—not just what it was.

"Third, use this as an opportunity to think critically about yourself. I loved writing my essay, because it gave me a forum to formulate my thoughts and talk about something that had previously only nagged at me from the back of my brain. And that's another thing—if you are stuck on what to write about, try thinking about something that makes you angry. It's great to write about what makes you happy, but I think identifying something that frustrates you and explaining why would probably lead to a more passionate piece."

—Ben L.

Finding Meaning

"Make sure your essay addresses what is important to you. If you find yourself struggling to write enough on your personal statement, you have picked the wrong topic to discuss. An essay that truly reflects who you are has to be about something so meaningful to you that it is difficult not to go over the word limit."

—Sumaya Quillian

20

WHAT I LEARNED FROM WRITING THE ESSAY

Shaped by Learning

"Writing about different experiences and people I care about made me realize that I have been shaped far more by the things I have learned than the qualities I naturally possess."

—*Sumaya Quillian*

Ready to Blossom in College

"I was obsessed with making my essay both true and beautiful. Insisting on both forced me to find the beautiful part of myself, the part that wanted to blossom in college (and certainly has). At the time, I thought it was about how I wanted to be a community organizer. Actually, the essay ended up being the story of my real education. Looking back on it now, I find it foreshadowed my trajectory in college and gives me confidence I'm on a good path. The essay also clearly marks that moment in my life, and lets me see I have learned a lot in college, since now it makes me cringe in its naiveté about my privilege."

—*Devney Hamilton*

Time Management Issues

"I guess I learned that I have serious issues with time management...but that was no surprise."

—Jasmine H.

A Different Kind of Writing

"I didn't really learn anything from writing my essays; however, I was surprised to find out how much about myself I revealed as I learned how to write. At first, I was unable to write about anything... I wasn't a club president. I wasn't the founder of any non-profit organization. I wasn't published in national newspapers. I was just an ordinary chump like most high school students are. As I learned how to write my paper, I realized that regardless of the lack of those amazing achievements, I was able to write a very personal essay of myself; an essay in which I could reveal every tidbit of myself I could. I have a feeling that many individuals who can write extremely well actually struggle on the personality aspect of the college essay. It's a totally different kind of writing and a grand awakening as well."

—Rob Resma

Responsibility

"My essays just seemed to come straight out of my head, and once they were on paper they felt and looked so familiar, that I did not feel as if I had made any grand revelation at all. What I learned later was that the whole process had forced me to take on a lot of responsibility, had made me more diligent and receptive to criticism than before, and that, in the end, just being the complete dork that I am got me into college, not some contrived image or persona. I also learned that I am somewhat of a risk taker, despite the fact that I had several copies, drafts and backups of all my admissions files on various computers, and that honesty pays off."

—Inès C. Gérard-Ursin

A Child's Free Spirit

"In writing this essay, I learned about the value of a child's free spirit and how we tend to forget simple life lessons as we grow up and conform to society rather than following our hearts."

—Katherine Christel

The Importance of Success

"I learned more than can be expressed. Most of my realizations didn't come from the actual essay though. I very well could have written an essay on writing college essays. The process of writing, editing until the words blurred together, actively searching for painful criticism, made me realize how much I really cared about success. Honestly, apart from my bakery and I suppose school as a whole, I've never worked at anything as hard as I did at writing those essays."

—*Christine Tataru*

Looking at Values

"I learned that I need to be more concise. I also learned that I do not need to communicate everything on my mind, just the essential facts. Writing the essay was reflective in a way and helped me begin looking at my values and who I am, but to be honest, those reflections came during college and not as much during the application process. I learned I need to be better at time management and organization in order to make sure that I accomplished all the drafts that I needed to. I also learned that I knew who I was at the time and that wherever I ended up getting into would be a place that I would make the most of, which was very reassuring especially since it was quite a gamble applying to Stanford."

—*Anonymous*

Not Getting Attached

"I learned to not attach myself to my own writing too much. Cutting my essays down to fit the word limit was so difficult, because I felt like I was losing style or voice with every edit. And as someone who has always prided herself on being a good writer, it was difficult to look at an essay and think, 'This isn't good enough. I should start over.' I ended up writing a total of 6 completely different essays for my Common App, so I also learned patience.

"Also, the night before the application was due, I almost had a breakdown and freaked out because I was sure that my essays weren't good enough....so I had to learn (and am still learning) how to stay calm."

—*Anonymous*

Reflecting on Upbringing

"As I was writing the essay, I became much more aware of how growing up in a rural area had affected my personal growth. As I first started writing, I thought it would be a useful thing to use, but by the time I was done with the application process I recognized how much growing up where I did influenced my own identity. As I put myself up against the image of what I believed Stanford students would be, the contrast was sharp and really help clarify how I thought about myself."

—*Jordan Haarsma*

Getting Comfortable about Opening Up

"I learned many things about myself from the experiences that I wrote about, but I also learned something from actually writing the essays. Every time I tell that acne story I learn a little bit more about myself, even years after it happened. Writing essays for applications made me realize that I really was comfortable with letting people know who I am, or at least the things that are really important to me. And branching off of that, writing those essays made me realize both what was most important to me, and exactly how important that event or time period was. It was also interesting writing the roommate essay because often times we write very differently than we speak and I had to overcome that to make it more personable. Writing essays was also a great tool for reminiscing! But I guess that's not necessarily learning..."

—*Brian Tashjian*

Appreciating Family

"I learned how much love I have for my parents and that I couldn't imagine being in any other kind of family. Also, despite having two moms, it was surprisingly hard to find things that were different between my everyday life and my friends'."

—*Reade Levinson*

Self-Reflection

"Writing my essay, I had to do a lot of self-reflection. I realized how much I had grown through my experience that I wrote about, and recognized the importance of really taking the time to review one's self."

—*Annelis Breed*

How Editing Others' Essays Helps

"I learned that editing essays for my peers was a great way to not only help them, but also to gain insight into how I could improve my own pieces. There are some things you don't notice about your own work until you're reading someone else's and something strikes you as off or out of place."

—*Sammi Rose Cannold*

Revising Is a Process

"I learned a lot about the process of revising. At first, the task of writing so many essays might seem tedious, but once you get started it gets progressively easier. But I realized that when you think you're 'done,' you still have to reread and share your work with your counselor or English teacher and it's important to stay open to changing various parts of your essay."

—*Cristina H. Mezgravis*

Self-Perception

"College essay writing takes a lot of introspective work, so yes, I learned a lot about myself and the way I perceive my character, values, and traits to be."

—*Anuj Patel*

Becoming More Concise

"I became a much more concise writer because of the admission essay writing process. It became clear pretty quickly that I was writing in a very flowery style and there were a lot of superfluous words and sentences. I think that I started to learn how to cut out the unnecessary or redundant stuff. But I'm still working on that."

—Jackie Botts

Aiming for a Concrete Description

"Because I was trying to very genuinely portray myself, I developed a language for how I thought of myself while writing my essay. While I had always been introspective and self-reflective, trying to put who I am to words, and to a very limited number of them at that, helped me to describe myself in more concrete ways than I had before."

—Anonymous

Being Patient with Yourself

"The whole college admissions process was an enormously educational experience for me. By virtue of the intensity of the application ordeal, I learned how to manage my time most efficiently and how to cope with my stress most effectively.

"Given the competitive environment that permeated my senior class, I learned how to finagle my way out of the uncomfortable interactions with peers who felt the need to offer me varying levels of encouragement and discouragement regarding the list of schools to which I was applying. When everyone I encountered seemed to have contradictory advice for me about where to go to college and how to get in, I learned to carefully evaluate my sources before accepting their authority.

"But writing the essay was arguably the biggest learning experience in that it illuminated for me how hastily and aggressively I tended to treat writing assignments. Because writing is a strong suit of mine, I was accustomed to generating literary gems in record time; I became frustrated with myself whenever I struggled to do so. This college essay did not come into being quickly, and thus it taught me about the importance of being patient with myself. I emerged from the essay-writing process having relinquished my unforgiving perfectionism a bit, trading it for a deliberate, methodical, persistent mindset. That new approach has served me incredibly well as I tackle and surmount the challenges that I encounter in college."

—Marisa G. Messina

A Critical Evaluation

"What started out as me grumbling and erratically venting my frustration turned into a critical evaluation of why I was frustrated, which in turn taught me how my struggle was ultimately worthwhile."

—*Ben L.*

Looking Behind

"Past memories impacted me much more than I had previously thought."

—*Rolando de la Torre, Jr.*

WRITE THE COLLEGE ADMISSION ESSAY THAT GETS YOU IN!

- 50 successful college essays—learn from the best
- Admission officers reveal exactly what colleges want to see in your admission essays
- 25 essay mistakes to avoid
- Complete instructions on crafting a powerful essay
- How to recycle your essay to save time
- Write the essay that will get you into your dream college

Accepted! 50 Successful College Admission Essays

ISBN: 978-1-61760-038-8

Price: $14.95

Get your copy at bookstores nationwide or from www.supercollege.com

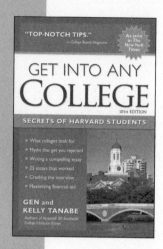

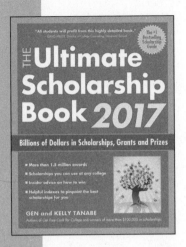

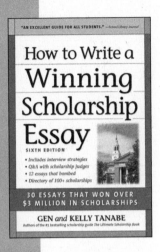

YOU WIN OR LOSE A SCHOLARSHIP WITH YOUR ESSAY AND INTERVIEW.

NOW YOU WILL LEARN HOW TO ACE BOTH!

- Complete instructions on crafting a powerful scholarship essay

- 30 money-winning essays that won $3 million in scholarships

- Scholarship judges reveal what separates a winner from a runner-up

- 12 essays that bombed and how to avoid their mistakes

- Master the interview with sample questions and answers

How to Write a Winning Scholarship Essay

ISBN: 978-1-61760-098-2

Price: $17.99

Get your copy at bookstores nationwide or from www.supercollege.com

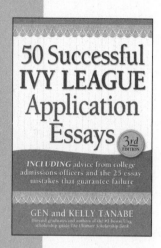

GET MORE TOOLS AND RESOURCES AT SUPERCOLLEGE.COM

Visit www.supercollege.com for more free resources on college admission, scholarships and financial aid. And apply for the SuperCollege Scholarship!

ABOUT THE AUTHORS

HARVARD GRADUATES GEN AND KELLY TANABE are the founders of SuperCollege and the award-winning authors of fourteen books including *The Ultimate Scholarship Book*, *The Ultimate Guide to America's Best Colleges*, *50 Successful Ivy League Application Essays*, *Accepted! 50 Successful College Admission Essays* and *1001 Ways to Pay for College*.

Together, Gen and Kelly were accepted to every school to which they applied, including all of the Ivy League colleges and Stanford, and won more than $100,000 in merit-based scholarships. They were able to leave Harvard debt-free and their parents guilt-free.

Gen and Kelly give workshops at high schools across the country. They have made hundreds of appearances on television and radio and have served as expert sources for respected publications including *U.S. News & World Report*, *USA Today*, *The New York Times*, *Chicago Sun-Times*, *New York Daily News*, *Chronicle of Higher Education* and *Seventeen*.

Gen grew up in Waialua, Hawaii. Between eating banana-flavored shave ice and basking in the sun, he was president of the Student Council, captain of the speech team and a member of the tennis team. A graduate of Waialua High School, he was the first student from his school to be accepted at Harvard. In college, Gen was chair of the Eliot House Committee and graduated magna cum laude with a degree in both History and East Asian Studies.

Kelly attended Whitney High School, a nationally ranked public high school in her hometown of Cerritos, California. She was the editor of the school newspaper, assistant editor of the yearbook and founder of a public service club to promote literacy. In college, she was the co-director of the HAND public service program and the brave co-leader of a Brownie Troop. She graduated magna cum laude with a degree in Sociology.

Gen, Kelly, their sons Zane and Kane and their dog Sushi live in Belmont, California.